The Japan
That Can Say
NO

Shintaro Ishihara

Translated by Frank Baldwin

FOREWORD BY EZRA F. VOGEL

A TOUCHSTONE BOOK
Published by Simon & Schuster
New York   London   Toronto   Sydney   Tokyo   Singapore

TOUCHSTONE
Simon & Schuster Building
Rockefeller Center
1230 Avenue of the Americas
New York, New York 10020

First Touchstone Edition 1992

Designed by Irving Perkins Associates
Manufactured in the United States of America

1   3   5   7   9   10   8   6   4   2

3   5   7   9   10   8   6   4   2 (pbk)

Library of Congress Cataloging-in-Publication Data

Ishihara, Shintaro, date
[Nō to ieru Nihon. English]
The Japan that can say no : why Japan will be first among equals /
Shintaro Ishihara.
p.   cm.
Translation of: Nō to ieru Nihon.
Edited and translated by Frank Baldwin. Cf. CIP data sheet.
Includes index.
1. United States—Relations—Japan.   2. Japan—Relations—United
States.   I. Baldwin, Frank.   II. Title.
E183.8.J3174213   1991
327.52073—dc20   90-22466
                                                                       CIP

ISBN 0-671-72686-2
0-671-75853-5 (pbk)

Portions of this work were previously published in Japan
by Kobunsha as *Nō To Ieru Nihon*.

Contents

Foreword

When Shintaro Ishihara's younger brother Yujiro died of cancer in 1987, Japan mourned as if the entire nation had lost a member of the family. As national public mourning, it was rivaled in the United States perhaps only by the public reaction to the death of John F. Kennedy or Robert Kennedy. In Japan, only the death of the Emperor received more public attention.

Shintaro and Yujiro were a remarkable pair, Shintaro, a writer and movie director, and Yujiro, an actor. In 1955, when Shintaro was only 21, his novel, *Taiyo no kisetsu (Season of the Sun)* won him the Bungaku newcomer's award and the Akutagawa Prize. His name became a household word. The novel was instantly made into a movie and proved immensely popular. Ishihara produced a string of novels of similar genre and when they too became movies, they were sensations. The star actor of these movies was his younger brother Yujiro. Known for his athletic build and cool style, he was sometimes referred to as "Japan's James Dean," but his popularity and influence far exceeded that of James Dean in America. Yujiro remained one of Japan's most popular actors until his death, and both he and his brother became the symbols of an alienated younger generation in Japan.

In the 1960s, as Japanese youth moved from the countryside to the city in search of new industrial jobs, the elders of Japan's Liberal Democratic Party (which is the conservative party) began to worry that the loss of the solid rural base of support might lead to its loss of power. They decided therefore to recruit some "tarento" (from "talent")—well-known popular figures, entertainers, novelists, actors, and television personalities—to run for the Diet. In 1968 one of their prize recruits was Shintaro Ishihara. In his first election, of all the thousands of candidates for the Diet, Ishihara received the largest number of votes of any candidate anywhere. Except for one brief period after he was defeated in his race for governor of Tokyo, he has remained in the Diet ever since.

Until recently, Japanese could assume that what they said to each other and wrote in their press would not get picked up by Americans, unable as they were to read Japanese. To be sure, some government publications like those of MITI on industrial policy, which were certain to be picked up by foreign governments, were written with the foreign reaction in mind. Among themselves, however, they could talk of American irrationality, pomposity, ignorance, and inferiority, assuming that it would not be noticed. Frank discussions disparaging non-yellow races and women who wanted to work or carry on political movements could appear in the Japanese press with little worry about America's different sensibilities. On the rare occasions that these everyday discussions were reported in the Western press, they were called "a slip."

Thus, when Akio Morita, chairman of Sony, gave a few talks for his friend Shintaro Ishihara to his political support groups, they could be printed and sell as many as a million copies under the title *"No" to ieru Nihon* ("A Japan That Can Say No," implying to the United States) with the assumption that the book would not be picked up in the United States. But it was, in an unauthorized translation, and it created an uproar in Washington and in the American press. Morita, to avoid any possible misunderstanding and to prevent any adverse commercial impact on Sony, refused to allow his portions of the original Japanese edition to be published in the authorized English translation. In fact, Morita had long been outspoken in English as well as Japanese, and the criticisms he made in the Japanese edition of American inefficiency and the poor quality of our products were not out of tune with the things he had long been saying directly to Americans.

Why should the book have received such attention in Washington? Because some Americans are concerned not only about the loss of American competitiveness but also about its implications that American defense is dependent on products the United States can not produce. Perhaps the most quoted passage of Ishihara's book was the comment that since Japan produces the computer chips needed by the Pentagon, the United States would be totally helpless if Japan refused to supply them and sold them to the U.S.S.R. instead, which could tip the balance in Sino-Soviet relations.

On this and other matters, Ishihara's book should not necessarily be read as a guide to how present-day Japanese politicians are likely to behave, but rather as a reflection of deep currents of popular Japanese thinking about the United States. Japan's political leaders are more pragmatic and more cautious than Ishihara. Indeed, in their Japanese context Ishihara's works still carry the flavor of a rebellion against the Japanese establishment. As Clyde Prestowitz or Pat Choate, seen by some as Japan-bashers, are really concerned with America getting its act together, so Ishihara is complaining less about the United States than about Japan's obsequious leaders who don't stand tall the way they should. And in that respect, he has his finger on the pulse of a growing segment of the Japanese population.

Americans need to read Ishihara's book to help us face the fact that Japan has surpassed us in industry, technology, and available capital. Not long before the pirated English versions of the Ishihara-Morita book made its rounds, an editor from a major American paper could travel around the globe and return to write a major five-part front-page story headlined "Is America Declining? Only Americans Think So." Anyone who speaks or reads Japanese or has been following Japanese opinion, or indeed following opinions in any major nation of East Asia, can only marvel at the Americans' capacity for self-deception.

The publication of Ishihara's book in English will, I hope, make such self-deception more difficult. Though we are beginning to acknowledge that Japan not only is stronger economically but that it looks down on America, the new method of self-deception is to say that it does not matter. America seems to have leadership for quick response to overseas military emergencies and for image management, but not for dealing with our underlying commercial inferiority which, as we begin to pay up our debts, will begin to take its toll. Perhaps America, too, needs an Ishihara, a very popular figure who could forthrightly tell our political leaders they should be standing tall, taking responsibility for restructuring the economy to promote long-term investment and preserve American manufacturing and high technology. One senses that if he were American, Ishihara would relish the role.

EZRA F. VOGEL
Harvard University

Introduction

SOME BOOKS suffer the slings and arrows of outrageous fortune. An American edition of this book was vilified before it was even published.

When *The Japan That Can Say No* was published in Japan, I thought there should also be an American edition, because it dealt with controversial aspects of the relationship between the two countries. As a politician and writer, I am convinced these ties are vital to both countries and the global community. I wanted my views and those of coauthor Akio Morita made available to the American public. I urged my longtime friend, Atsushi Matsushita, the editor at Kobunsha who had originally suggested the book, to prepare a synopsis quickly for an American publisher.

Meanwhile, it was clear that the Japanese edition, a blend of statements by and dialogue between Morita and myself, was in many respects insufficient. The somewhat fragmentary nature of my part especially was liable to cause misunderstanding. As I began preparing supplementary material, Matsushita was arranging for a sample translation that would give American publishers the flavor of the book. Then disaster struck. Perhaps my running for president of the ruling Liberal Democratic party in August 1989 sparked interest in my views. Whatever the cause, a pirated translation suddenly surfaced in Washington, D.C., and Morita and Ishihara were the talk of the town, particularly on Capitol Hill.

In January 1990, I discovered that the Pentagon's Defense Advanced Research Projects Agency was behind the piracy—one would think the Department of Defense would want a complete and accurate manuscript. The illicit version was full of mistakes, some laughable and some very serious, and many parts of the original were omitted. The bowdlerized mess was so bad that it made meaningful discussion of the issues Morita and I raised impossible.

I encouraged Kobunsha to proceed with an authorized translation, but coauthor Morita declined to participate in an American edition, and I was unable to change his mind. Our situations are different, of course. As a businessman, he must consider the consequences of adverse publicity, while I am free to speak for myself. To make my half of the original long enough for a book, I began to expand upon my positions with additional chapters. Politics, however, intervened. The Diet (parliament) was dissolved in January and I ran for reelection to the lower house in February. Only after the campaign was I finally able to return to the manuscript.

Having no excuses or apologies to make for what I said in the original, it appears here in its entirety as Part One. Small changes have been made but only for reasons of style and clarity. These additions are closed in brackets in the text. Deletions, which were made for clarity or to avoid repetition, are indicated thus: [...]. The deletion indicated on page 48 consists of four paragraphs that now begin Chapter 8 in Part Two; this change was made because I wanted to combine two separate discussions of these points. Thus, in Part One, there are no differences of substance between this translation and the original Japanese edition. Part Two has been developed from articles originally written for Japanese magazines, and revised for this edition.

I offer this book to American readers with the recognition that too much is at stake for Japan and the United States to drift apart. To stay together, we have to understand each other. And a frank, sincere dialogue is the key, even if our tempers flare occasionally. For many cultural reasons, Japanese are not used to freewheeling debate. Uncomfortable in confrontational situations, we try to avoid a clash of opinions. But Japanese must realize that silence is self-destructive and reticence can harm a friendship. The differences between Japanese and Americans often lead to misinterpretation and stereotyping. A mutual dose of honesty and clarity is the antidote. I hope this book will be a catalyst for candor.

The 1990s promise to be a period of breathtaking political and economic change. The Japanese people must take stock, fairly and objectively, of themselves and their relationship with the United States. The United States, in turn, must take a new look at its relationship with Japan. Both countries will benefit from a closer and truly equal partnership. I am confident we can overcome the current strains, the worst of the postwar period, and forge a closer alliance.

Part One

CHAPTER 1

A New National Consciousness

EVERY MONTH, the cabinet and senior officials of Japan's Liberal Democratic party (LDP) receive a joint economic briefing by a bureau chief from the Economic Planning Agency (EPA) and the governor of the Bank of Japan. The briefing is given before a cabinet meeting, which, when the Diet is in session, starts at 9:00 A.M., or sometimes even at 8:00 A.M. I hate to get up early, but, rubbing the sleep out of my eyes, I always went to these briefings. The reports were almost identical every time; most of the ministers dozed off.

It seemed like a meaningless ritual to me. After all, since the early 1980s, the government had championed administrative and fiscal reforms to deregulate the economy and streamline administration. So I suggested to Chief Cabinet Secretary Keizo Obuchi that the briefings were a waste of time and should be discontinued. He tended to agree, he said, but added that they were the only chance for some LDP officials to participate in a cabinet-level meeting. To abolish the sessions would slight them.

A Nation of ETs

The briefings took place when Noboru Takeshita was prime minister (1987–89); at the time I was transport minister. I used to sit there and listen as an EPA official intoned the trade statistics: "This month, just as last month, the current-account surplus continued to decline steadily." In other words, he was telling us that Japan's trade position was worsening and that was wonderful. Some of the participants muttered "I see" and underlined that sentence in the report.

During one briefing, I leaned over to Seiroku Kajiyama, the home affairs minister and a close friend, and said, "I think Japan's days are numbered. This guy says business is bad and that's good, and everybody nods in agreement and marks the sentence."

"They're just words. Their meaning has changed, that's all," Kajiyama murmured.

I do not know exactly what he meant, but I suppose he was saying our perspective on Japan's economy had changed. According to the highly publicized 1986 Maekawa Report, Japan's huge trade surplus is a dangerous liability, and the economy must be restructured to shift from export-led growth to expansion based on domestic demand. Leaving aside whether the report's conclusions should be regarded as holy writ, Japan's economy *is* changing. Big, powerful smokestack industries such as steel and shipbuilding are giving way to lean, compact, knowledge-intensive fields such as software, computers, and semiconductors.

In human terms, if we heard that a tall, muscular man was going to be "re-sized," it would be cause for alarm. Nevertheless, today, everybody—the Maekawa advisory group, economists, politicians—is saying that Japanese industry must be restructured and the economy led by the knowledge-intensive sector.

Is that good for Japan? Will we be able to sustain our prosperity? People will no longer do hard physical labor. They will not make things in factories and machine shops, get their hands dirty on assembly lines, or sweat in front of blast furnaces. I am not denigrating the mental effort of writing a computer program or developing a new technology. These are important jobs. But all brain and no brawn cannot be good for the country. Everyone an egghead? History is not encouraging; no such nation has ever flourished. Perhaps an unprecedented experiment has been thrust upon Japan. Be that as it may, I don't think we should blithely assume we are a chosen people and accept this destiny.

Figuratively speaking, I sometimes wonder if Japan is not becoming a nation of ETs, that charming visitor from outer space with an oversized head and spindly arms and legs. If that is the course of evolution, ET-like human beings will appear first in Japan. That would explain why we did so poorly at the Seoul Olympics, winning only a handful of gold medals. Maybe that miserable performance indicates that we are acquiring an unconventional, sophisticated temperament and life-style. As a nation, however, we would be better off if our Olympic athletes won a basket of medals and the younger generation did strenuous work. [Still, there is no question that Japan's trump card is its advanced technology.]

Although the 1987 INF Treaty limiting intermediate-range nuclear forces was a momentous event, the United States and Soviet Union did not act from a belated realization that nuclear weapons endanger humankind and, therefore, can never be used. Some observers, of course, believe the arms limitation talks succeeded because Washington and Moscow were motivated by such a lofty purpose, but I find the explanation elsewhere.

The accuracy of both intermediate-range and intercontinental ballistic missiles (ICBMs) depends on the quality of their computers. The ICBMs are multiple independently targetable reentry vehicles (MIRVs) that launch eight or nine hydrogen warheads, each capable of hitting a different target. Many of the warheads are decoys that lead antiballistic missiles on a merry chase until they are hit and destroyed. The real warheads take evasive action by varying speed, looping, free-falling, and slipping sideways. Then they lock onto their targets, which have been previously identified by spy satellites.

The Soviet Union and the United States each has a priority hit list. Moscow's first-strike objective is the retaliatory missile launch complex at Vandenberg Air Force Base, California, where the reinforced-concrete missile silos have walls fifty to sixty meters thick and are built far underground. The silos can withstand strong earthquakes; their only vulnerability is to a hydrogen-bomb explosion. But even a hydrogen bomb must score a direct hit to destroy the missile inside.

Soviet missiles can hit within sixty meters of such a target. The Americans can do a little better—within fifteen meters— and they have been trying to get closer. The increasing sophistication of defensive missiles means the MIRVed warheads must follow more complex courses, and to do this they need ever more powerful computers to process information instantaneously. These weapons systems use fourth-generation computers; the so-called fifth-generation, presently under development; will require multimegabit semiconductors. While U.S. companies may already have the technological know-how for the advanced chips, only Japanese electronics firms have the mass-production and quality-control capability to supply the multimegabit semiconductors for the weapons systems and other equipment.

In short, without using new-generation computer chips made in Japan, the U.S. Department of Defense cannot guarantee the precision of its nuclear weapons. If Japan told Washington it would no longer sell computer chips to the United States, the Pentagon would be totally helpless. Furthermore, the global military balance could be completely upset if Japan decided to sell its computer chips to the Soviet Union instead of the United States. (Some Americans say that if we contemplated such action, U.S. forces would reoccupy Japan.)

Japan now has a decisive technological advantage. I believe that Ronald Reagan, Mikhail Gorbachev, and their advisers realized the absurdity of the situation—that the accuracy of their nuclear arsenals depended on Japanese chips—and agreed to call off the arms race.

A Pentagon report corroborates my belief that Japan holds the trump card in the nuclear arms race. A report from the Defense Science Board's task force on semiconductor dependency reveals U.S. apprehension about Japanese technology, especially semiconductors. The report accurately notes U.S. weaknesses and Japanese superiority in microchips, adding that if the situation were to continue the United States would be at Japan's beck and call. So far, only the U.S. president and a small number of officials have seen the report; if made public, the report would trigger widespread alarm.

Among its conclusions, the report noted that U.S. military power has been heavily dependent on technological superiority, particularly electronics equipment. "Semiconductors are the key to leadership in electronics," the report says, and "competitive, high-volume production is the key to leadership in semiconductors." But, the report continues, "High volume production is supported by the commercial market."

And unlike Japan, the United States lacks a market for the wide variety of products that use semiconductors, such as rice cookers. The report concludes: "Leadership in commercial volume production is being lost by the U.S. semiconductor industry. . . . Semiconductor technology leadership, which in this field is closely coupled to manufacturing leadership, will soon reside abroad. U.S. defense will soon depend on foreign sources for state-of-the-art technology in semiconductors. The Task Force views this as an unacceptable situation."

The "foreign sources" referred to in the report are Japanese companies. It is my impression that the mood in Washington is nearly hysterical because the linchpin of U.S. military might—semiconductor technology—is held by another country and it is not European but Asian: Japan. Pentagon officials are also probably worried that the shift of manufacturing leadership abroad makes it easier for the Soviets to get their hands on computer systems and microchips.

The Reagan administration's sanctions against Toshiba in 1987 were part of this hysteria. A Toshiba subsidiary violated a COCOM (Coordinating Committee for Export Control) ban on high-tech sales to Communist countries by selling precision milling machines to the Soviet Union. The Pentagon charged that subsequent retooling made Soviet nuclear-powered submarines more difficult to detect. There was no legal basis for action against Toshiba, and there was no causal relationship between the sale and quieter Soviet submarines. [Nevertheless, sanctions were imposed.]

[The United States does indeed have cause for concern, if not hysteria.] The one-megabyte chip used in computer memory banks has a million circuits on a silicon base one-third the size of the nail on my little finger. This vital component is made only in Japan. Japanese manufacturers almost completely control the market. The United States has the know-how but lacks the engineers and technicians to produce these chips. Without an integrated development and manufacturing system, this precious knowledge is wasted.

In search of cheap labor, U.S. companies have moved their production offshore and make 256-bit chips in Southeast Asia. Nevertheless, the U.S. semiconductor industry now lags more than five years behind Japan's, and is falling farther back. Some high-tech basic research requires state-of-the-art computers. Breakthroughs occur in a virtuous circle: It takes a highly advanced computer to create an even more advanced computer. Technology is so structured that once a gap opens, it keeps widening.

The United States is desperate because electronics are the mainstay of national strength, including military power. For example, to decide which of the new materials would be best for an aircraft capable of flying at Mach 2, engineers use computer-aided design (CAD) simulation. An ordinary computer would take forty years to come up with the answer; the newest and fastest computers can provide the data in one year. With almost complete control over the one-megabyte chips such computers use, Japan is in a very strong position.

High-Tech Leadership: The National Awakening

As ideological confrontation fades, remote areas of China and the Soviet Union's Siberian region may be the next great centers of economic development.

The technology exists to connect these inaccessible zones to outside markets: new high-speed train systems—known as maglev for "magnetic levitation"—for example. The maglev trains float on superconducting magnets and are propelled forward by coils set in the floor of the guideway. Japan and

West Germany are the leaders in this field, and Japan is far ahead of the Germans, both theoretically and in actual test performances. Daunted by three technical obstacles, the Germans have given up on superconductivity, but our engineers have solved the puzzles.

To give one example, West Germany's maglev rises only eight millimeters off the track. Japan's version, using superconductivity, floats ten centimeters above the track. Both can easily travel five hundred kilometers per hour. Neither the United States nor the Soviet Union has been working on space-age rail transportation.

Provided there is a consensus among Japanese business and political leaders that enables us to use this technology effectively, we can meet the incredible challenges thrust upon Japan. [The same is true of our other technological breakthroughs.] If we make the right choices at every stage, I believe we can [retain our high-tech leadership]. It all depends on the acumen of our political leaders.

In the 1970s, Akio Morita formed a study group, called the Jiyu Shakai Kenkyukai, to bring together up-and-coming politicians and business executives. I have been privileged to be a member of that group. Each year, Morita has invited Henry Kissinger, the former U.S. secretary of state, a personal acquaintance of his, to speak to the group. A few years ago, Kissinger told us that although it was a remote possibility, Japan might become a military superpower. I do not think he was suggesting Japan would be so foolish as to acquire ICBMs and build battleships like the *Yamato*, the behemoth of World War II. I think he probably meant that Japan's technological superiority gave it a decisive role no matter what space-based weapons systems Washington or Moscow created.

To use the technology card in the high-stakes poker game of international politics, Japan's leaders must have skill and guts.

But I wonder if any of them can see Japan's new standing in the proper historical perspective. [. . .] Like any good poker player, sometimes we have to take risks and at other times be cautious. The game is under way. Japan is an economic and high-tech superpower; we have no choice but to play.

If we want to stay in the game, however, many of our institutions must be reformed, including the tax system. We have not quite gotten over the experience of defeat and occupation. Nevertheless, I am pleased that attitudes are changing, albeit slowly.

In the last forty years, many countries have gone through profound transformations. De-Stalinization forced the Soviets to question the infallibility of their political leadership. Mao Zedong launched the Cultural Revolution in a bid to root out bourgeois values. The Vietnam War made many Americans see their country in a different light. But in Japan, the postwar mentality has lingered to the present day. Our preeminence in technology must help us achieve a new consciousness without traumatic convulsions. Fresh perceptions are the sine qua non of a genuinely mature society.

CHAPTER 2

Racial Prejudice: The Root Cause of Japan-Bashing

IN APRIL 1987, about five days after Congress imposed sanctions on Japanese semiconductor makers, I visited Washington, D.C. The mood was venomously hostile. In conversations with several members of the Senate and House of Representatives whom I knew well, I said matter-of-factly that I thought racial prejudice was behind the trade friction between our two countries, and I cited several specific examples. American politicians get upset about such terms as racism, but those I spoke to finally conceded, with a wry smile, that I had a point. Interestingly, at first they had insisted prejudice was not a factor, and then said it might stem from the Pacific War. In my opinion, lingering distrust from World War II could not be the only reason.

Westerners, subconsciously at least, take great pride in

having created the modern age. During my meetings with politicians in Washington, I said, "I admit that Caucasians created modern civilization, but what bothers me is you seem to think that heritage makes you superior. In the thirteenth century, however, the Mongols under Genghis Khan and his successors overran Russia and eastern Europe, reaching almost to Vienna and Venice. Mongol armies destroyed every army and fortress in their path, plundering and raping. Caucasians adopted Mongol-style haircuts and shaved eyebrows, and even the Mongols' bandy-legged gait. Just as Orientals of today are crazy about the clothing and hairstyles of the Beatles, Michael Jackson, and Sting, Occidentals of Genghis Kahn's time copied Mongolian ways. Even women liked the new styles."

Eventually, the Mongol empire disintegrated, but some people trace Western fear of Asians—the concept of the yellow peril—to the slaughter and pillage committed by the Mongol forces. Whatever the reason, Japanese should not forget that Caucasians are prejudiced against Orientals.

The U.S. Choice: Racism or World Leadership

American prejudice was clearly evident in a discussion I had with a senior U.S. Navy officer. The U.S. Navy places a powerful sonar unit that can detect unusual objects on the bows of civilian tankers and container ships. Called the Amber System, its purpose is to locate nuclear submarines. The sonar cannot distinguish between U.S. and Soviet subs; it just flashes a sighting report to the Pentagon. The U.S. Navy knows the location of its own subs and can determine if the object is friend or foe.

I suggested to the officer that the Amber System be installed on Japanese merchant vessels, which sail all the tanker and cargo routes and have well-trained, reliable crews. Japan could collect raw intelligence data for the U.S. Navy to analyze. The officer said that Japan's help would not be necessary. I pressed the idea, noting that Soviet subs outnumbered the U.S. underwater fleet. He replied that he could not ask Japan's merchant marine to participate. If West Germany or Britain made such an offer, I asked, would you install the Amber System on their merchant vessels? The officer candidly answered that the Pentagon would.

Americans feel that they cannot trust Japan. We cannot decode the sonar signals, but still they choose not to ask us to collect the data. U.S. admirals would probably even ask the Russians before they asked the Japanese! The Japanese people should be aware of how deeply biased Americans are.

In World War II, for example, the United States bombed German cities and killed many civilians but did not use atomic bombs on the Germans. U.S. planes dropped them on us because we are Japanese. Every American I mention this to denies that race was the reason, but the fact remains that nuclear bombs were dropped on Hiroshima and Nagasaki. We should never forget this. The same virulent racism underlies trade friction with the United States.

American racism stems from pride in cultural superiority. But because the United States is an arriviste, there is an arrogance that distorts the American view of other cultures, particularly those of Asia. Given the state of American education, however, students cannot get a proper cross-cultural perspective. Americans should know, as the early Portuguese and Spanish missionaries wrote, that Japan had a highly advanced civilization by the mid-sixteenth century. In the Tokugawa period (1603–1867), more than 20,000 private schools throughout Japan taught reading and writing, a standard of school attendance and literacy without parallel for the time. Even townspeople could write the Japanese syllabaries and as many as 2,000 Chinese characters. An excellent mail service delivering letters, freight, and cash extended from Edo (now Tokyo) to Kyushu. Local libraries all across Japan have collections of correspondence and other materials from this period. But if you try to tell Americans about Japan's past accomplishments, they are so conceited about Western civilization that they get bored.

Today, the modern era is in its terminal phase. An awareness of its imminent demise has made Americans, the most powerful Caucasians since World War II, increasingly emotional, almost hysterical, about Japan. Both societies are in a similar transitional phase, which makes the rivalry more intense. The kind of trade friction that exists between Japan and the United States would not occur if a West Germany, Britain, or Australia had achieved our economic power and standing. When pressed about racism, many Americans honestly admit their feelings. But that is not enough. They must purge themselves of bigotry. Given the power and importance of the United States, Americans especially should understand that the world is at one of those moments of epochal change. Technology, manufacturing, and economic power are gradually shifting from the West to the East. Whether that means the Age of the Pacific has dawned, I do not know. But I am certain that despite the ethnic and racial diversity of the U.S. population, persistent discrimination by the white power elite against Japan and other Asian countries will undermine U.S. leadership of the free world.

As the modern civilization created by Caucasians comes to an end in the last decade of the twentieth century, we are on the verge of a new genesis. Japanese, and Americans, too, are shaping this age. American politicians must explain to the

American people that times have changed. In fact, however, other U.S. opinion leaders—businessmen, for example—are more aware of the profound transition under way than the political leadership. Americans, with their scant few centuries of history, have never experienced the shift from one major historical period to another. They emerged as the premier world power only decades ago, toward the end of the modern era. That Japan, an Oriental country, is about to supplant them in some major fields is what annoys the Americans so much.

Cosmopolitan Japanese

Japanese, of course, must also prepare for the new era. They must become more cosmopolitan and less insular. Sony chairman Akio Morita, proud and confident of his company's excellent products, personifies this urbanity. Other Japanese as well, buoyed by our technological prowess and flourishing culture, should be more self-assured. We do not have to be arrogant, but if we continue to feel inferior, Japan cannot be the mainspring of the new genesis. To bear the great responsibilities that lie ahead, Japanese must change their attitudes and self-image.

One group badly in need of a new outlook is Japan's diplomatic corps. With the exception of the younger personnel and some extraordinary officers, our diplomats as a whole are responsible for much of the misunderstanding about Japan. Their behavior overseas perpetuates negative stereotypes.

Many years ago, I spent a month visiting a Japanese ambassador, a wonderful person and an avid golfer. One day we played eighteen holes together at the best local country club. Afterward I said, "Let's have a drink in the club bar." "No, I would rather drink at home," he replied. His standoffish refusal to mingle was seen as unfriendliness by club members. Perhaps Japanese can only really relax with other Japanese or their families, but such clannish behavior prevents us from becoming cosmopolitan. In any case, that country club later rejected applications from local managers of Mitsui & Company and Mitsubishi Corporation. After the experience with the ambassador, it did not want any more Japanese who would use the links but not fraternize with the members.

Some diplomats are even worse. One ambassador wrote a shameful book that revealed his own sense of inferiority. He actually said that Japanese are as physically unattractive as Pygmies. People like him should not be in the foreign service.

The Foreign Ministry's institutional deference toward the U.S. government was evident in an incident involving a U.S. Navy guided-missile destroyer. On November 9, 1988, the U.S.S. *Towers* conducted a firing drill in crowded Tokyo Bay that the ministry tried to cover up. The *Towers* can fire thirty-six thirty-two-kilogram shells per minute with a maximum range of twenty-three kilometers. According to the U.S. Navy, the destroyer fired "non-explosive, sand-filled projectiles." In any case, the rounds landed near the Maritime Safety Agency's 3,231-ton patrol vessel *Uraga*, which the *Towers* used as a hypothetical target. Direct hits probably would have badly damaged the *Uraga* or sunk a small fishing boat. A U.S. TV news report said that if a foreign warship had taken target practice in the Narrows off New York City, Americans would be outraged. It was an intolerable act.

I was minister of transport at the time. The Foreign Ministry's position was that "these things happen," and the government should delay making the incident public. This pusillanimous attitude infuriated me. I said the media would get the story anyway, so I would release it on my responsibility. A U.S. destroyer had conducted firing practice not only in Japanese territorial waters but in one of the world's busiest maritime crossroads. The U.S. Navy had clearly violated Japanese sovereignty. Someone at the Defense Agency compared it to firing a pistol on the Ginza at high noon. The U.S. military probably believes such actions are permissible, because they are defending Japan under the Japan-U.S. Security Treaty. But I have to think that the watchdog, in this instance, had become a mad dog.

I use that analogy because when Etsusaburo Shiina, former vice-president of the LDP, was foreign minister in the 1960s, he referred to the U.S. forces in Japan as "the honorable Mr. Watchdog." Instead of criticizing Shiina for such an expression, Foreign Ministry officials should speak up to the Americans in cases like the *Towers* incident. Tell the U.S. Navy: "No target practice in our territorial waters." If the Japanese do not respond firmly when circumstances warrant it, the Americans will not respect us and their racial prejudices will deepen. Japanese should realize that we have finally reached the position, thanks to our technology, where we can and must make an enormous contribution to U.S. security. Some Americans already understand this. It is the reality of our bilateral relationship today.

CHAPTER 3

Who Is Really "Unfair"?

THE MORE stridently U.S. officials charge that Japan's trading practices are "unfair," the more I want to tell them to calm down and do their homework. As transport minister, I had a heated exchange with Secretary of Commerce William Verity because he did not know what he was talking about.

The U.S. Congress had complained that large-scale public works projects in Japan were closed to American contractors. In fact, however, at the time, only one U.S. construction company had a license to operate in Japan and one other's application was pending. The Americans claimed that Japanese regulations and red tape were impenetrable. My own feeling was that every country has its particular practices and customs, and the foreign businessman has to adjust. Bowing to pressure from Washington, the Japanese government had reluctantly allowed U.S. construction companies to participate in part of the work at Haneda Airport, though the contracts had already been awarded. Verity was in Tokyo partly to express appreciation for that decision.

At our meeting, I warned Verity not to expect special treatment for U.S. firms again. I mentioned, however, that airport buildings and high-speed train stations in Japan were designed in the worst kind of complacent, provincial taste. I thought foreign architects could do a better job. I had recently been to the New Tokyo International Airport and had seen that the pillars were unpainted. They were just coated with a rust preventive. I told an official the pillars were unsightly and to have them painted immediately. "You never noticed them before?" he asked. "The pillars have been that way since the airport opened in 1978." When I asked why there was a grotesque variation of red, white, and black pillars, he said it was for contrast. "Whose idea was it?" I asked. Without a trace of irony, the hapless man said, "The painting contractor."

There is no decent cocktail lounge at the airport either. Many travelers feel a little tense before boarding a flight and relieved when they reach their destination. A drink helps at both ends. In airports abroad, there are convenient little bars where passengers can have a drink while awaiting departure, even during the daytime. That is one of the pleasures of taking a trip.

American Hypocrisy

[In my opinion, the design and the facilities of the New Tokyo International Airport could be greatly improved.] Verity understood and nodded in agreement. Then, as you would expect from a secretary of commerce, he changed the subject to the New Kansai International Airport, which is under construction in Osaka Bay, saying he was glad that U.S. firms had been permitted to bid on the project. He should have left it at that, but the secretary went on to request that upon completion of the facility, scheduled for 1992, U.S. carriers be allowed as many flights from it as Japanese airlines. I rejected the idea out of hand. His face flushed with anger, Verity asked for an explanation.

The Japan-U.S. Aviation Agreement dates from the Occupation period and is very unfair, particularly on landing rights and fly-on rights to other countries. U.S. airlines can fly through Japan to any other destination; there are no restrictions. The only continuation service granted Japanese carriers at U.S. airports under the 1952 agreement is San Francisco–New York–Europe, not a lucrative route. In fact, our airlines do not fly it. At the 1982 meeting between Ronald Reagan and Yasuhiro Nakasone, the United States granted Japan two flights weekly from San Francisco to São Paulo and Rio de Janeiro. In 1985, Washington finally approved nine flights a week for Nippon Cargo Airlines on the Tokyo–San Francisco–New York route. In return, the Reagan administration insisted upon and got the rights for a U.S. air freight carrier to off-load cargo in Japan and transfer it to small and medium cargoliners for delivery to Manila, Taipei, Seoul, and other Asian capitals. Meanwhile, the U.S. side rejected our request for cargo flights to Chicago.

In the United States there are nineteen international airports compared with Japan's three—Tokyo, Nagoya, and Osaka, although admittedly the United States is much larger. There is also a great disparity in the number of flights to each country. As of November 1988, Japan had 204.5 passenger flights per month, far fewer than the 371 by U.S. airlines, and 60 cargo flights versus 170 by U.S. freight carriers. The agreement is grossly unfair. U.S. aviation experts appreciate how favorable the status quo is. Repeated Japanese initiatives to

renegotiate the terms have never gotten off the ground. Yet
Verity wanted even more concessions!

When I explained all this to him, he said he was unaware of
the history of the agreement. I told him a cabinet secretary
who didn't know this background was not qualified to discuss
the number of U.S. flights to be allowed at Osaka Airport. A
State Department official was present at our meeting, so I
suggested Verity check with him. Obviously upset, Verity
asked the aide if the bilateral agreement was really that unfair. The foreign service officer, an honest man, admitted that
it was. Verity, who had expected support, seemed embarrassed. The U.S. secretary of commerce and a State Department official were at loggerheads in front of Japan's transport
minister! From this side of the Pacific, we tend to think of the
U.S. government as a powerful monolith. That is not the case.
Within it there are differing views and conflicts of interest, for
example between the Commerce Department and the Office
of the U.S. Trade Representative.

There was really bad blood between Verity and Clayton
Yeutter, the U.S. trade representative, with each one bad-
mouthing the other. Verity never said anything negative
about Yeutter in my presence—just in case, I suppose,
Yeutter had sent along a subordinate to keep an eye on his
fellow cabinet member. After my sharp disagreement with
Verity, Yeutter's man winked at me as if to say, "Hang in
there." I smiled, thinking to myself, "The United States is not
so united after all."

Japanese Creativity

While critical of other nations, Americans are blind to their
own unfair practices and one-sided opinions. For example,

Americans assert that Japanese are "just imitators." But as Akio Morita has amply shown, the charge that Japan has only improved on and commercialized American technology is a canard. Yet many Japanese believe it. In fact, we have a long, distinguished record of creativity. The contributions of our scientists and engineers are increasingly acknowledged abroad.

Westerners are becoming more appreciative of Japanese originality in cultural fields, too. The French used to ignore Japanese literature. In recent years, however, they reportedly have begun to hold our belles lettres in higher esteem, thanks to Japanese high technology. Many French engineers studying the Japanese language in order to scan technical reports also read modern Japanese novels and find them fascinating. It is worth noting that this acclaim comes from the French scientific community, not writers and translators, as is usually the case. Literature is a superbly creative art, an act of the imagination.

We should not be daunted by American charges that Japanese are just copiers. Confidence in our inherent gift for originality in the arts and sciences is well merited. Just to cite one example, Sony engineers transformed American notions about the radio. In the old days, the whole family had to share a large console in the living room. There was much disagreement over whose favorite program would be listened to. Sony's transistorized models changed all that. Now [radios are much more compact and much less expensive, and] a personal radio is almost a constitutional right in the United States. Sony's inventive engineers deserve credit for opening up a whole new market. It was a simple concept, but then many great ideas are.

Creativity in Japan is not limited to a scientific or cultural elite. You see it everywhere, among people from all walks of life. Our supremacy in high technology stems from an alert, innovative labor force. Everyone in a company contributes, from top to bottom. One genius is not enough. You need excellent engineers and technicians to take an idea or laboratory discovery to the factory and turn out quality manufactured goods. The low rate of defective products shows the outstanding level of technical ability in Japan. Excellence in manufacturing bespeaks a crack work force.

The Boeing Case

A few years ago, the accident-plagued Boeing Company, in an effort to restore public confidence, announced the results of a study of its manufacturing processes. Weaknesses were being rapidly rectified, the company said. Retrained factory supervisory staff would soon reach an acceptable level, but shortcomings in line workers remained. Asked how long it would take before blue-collar personnel attained the desired standard, the head of Boeing's Seattle factory said seven years. Think of that for a moment. For seven years we would have to fly in Boeing planes that are probably defective and should not be in the air!

Then on August 12, 1985, a Japan Airlines Boeing 747 SR jumbo jet crashed in Gumma Prefecture, killing 520 people. The worst single-plane accident in aviation history, it was due to Boeing's shoddy workmanship. Japanese police even interrogated JAL and Ministry of Transport inspectors, and the men faced possible indictment for not discovering Boeing's foul-up. But under U.S. law, an aircraft maker is not prosecuted for criminal negligence. The logic behind this is that rather than punish a few individuals, the public interest is better served if they candidly describe what happened and a recurrence is prevented. The U.S. legal system assumes that unless people are given immunity, they will not tell the truth. Given the scale of this accident, that premise was unfathomable, not only to the families and friends of the victims but to most Japanese.

A Japanese police report showed that four Boeing employees were responsible, and the company admitted their error caused the tragedy. The 747 crashed because of faulty repairs to its tail assembly, which had been damaged in a hard landing in 1978. Standard procedures called for a splice plate to be riveted between two bulkhead panels. Boeing mechanics muffed this simple task. The bulkhead was bolted on both ends, but the bolts only went through two of the three thicknesses. The weakened section snapped, damaging the hydraulic system, and the pilots lost control of the plane. Five hundred twenty people died because Boeing workers were so incompetent or careless that they could not securely fasten a three-ply bulkhead. Such shoddy performance by a Japanese corporation is unthinkable.

In response to Reagan administration demands, Japanese firms have purchased semiconductors from U.S. manufacturers. When Japanese complained about the absurdly high defect rate, American executives said they were the only unsatisfied end-users. The implication was that our companies were somehow wrong for insisting on quality. That response made me wonder if the United States is not finished as a great country. But perhaps there is still hope. In the last few years, the U.S. semiconductor industry has improved its defect rate to only five or six times the ratio in Japan, down from ten times higher.

A Japanese Worth Ethic

I recently heard an inspiring story that shows why Japanese companies outperform their U.S. counterparts. It concerned a dedicated female employee at NEC Corporation's Kumamoto semiconductor factory. For some reason, the plant turned out a good many more defective chips than any other NEC facility. The factory manager and employees met daily to try to fix the problem. They took corrective action and tried novel solutions without success; they could not reduce the reject rate below a certain point. Everyone was puzzled as to why only Kumamoto could not meet company-wide norms.

One day the heroine of this story was walking to work and stopped at the railroad crossing in front of the factory while a very long freight train passed. She felt the ground vibrating as the heavy cars rumbled by and suddenly it occurred to her that this shaking might be the culprit. Later, on the job, when a train passed she felt no vibration. Nevertheless, thinking that perhaps the precision machinery might be affected, she told the foreman. Shortly afterward, the factory manager ordered a deep ditch dug all along the side of the plant facing the tracks and had it filled with water. Eureka! The moatlike barrier absorbed the vibration and the defect rate dropped sharply. The woman was only eighteen years old, but she took pride in her job and NEC. She cared enough to think about a company problem on her own time. That kind of work ethic reflects the superiority of Japan's school system.

The industrialized capitalist countries are engaged in severe economic competition, if not a trade war. Private companies square off toe to toe. Sometimes, in the heat of the contest, their cheering sections—government officials and politicians—vilify opponents, yell "unfair," and demand new rules. Japan has quietly endured this rhetorical crescendo from the United States for years. We cannot remain silent forever. It is time to speak out.

CHAPTER 4

Stand Up to U.S. Threats

ABOUT 1987, the United States began using a new tactic against Japan. Given Gorbachev's popularity in the West and the reduced threat from the "evil empire," Japan-bashing became even more frequent. It was open season on Tokyo as one politician after another made wild, emotional attacks. [. . .] Instead of carefully weighing all the facts, Congress went off half-cocked. Several members, for example, smashed a Toshiba radio–cassette player to bits with sledgehammers on the steps of the Capitol. That was a disgraceful act.

The Technology Card

During my April 1987 visit to Washington, politicians hinted at a détente with the Soviet Union, implying that the two Caucasian races would soon be on much friendlier terms, leaving Japan out in the cold. Our foreign policy makers must not be intimidated by this absurd threat. We control the high technology on which the military power of both countries rests. Unfortunately, Japan has not used the technology card skillfully. We have the power to say no to the United States, but we have not exercised that option. We are like a stud poker player with an ace in the hole who habitually folds his hand.

The American lawmakers I met with bristled when I said they had no credibility because Congress, ignoring administration goals, so often acted erratically and self-indulgently. "The best example is Prohibition," I said. "No legislative assembly worthy of the name would pass such a law." They laughed with embarrassment.

The semiconductor dispute between Japan and the United States deteriorated to sanctions because we did not reject U.S. demands at the crucial stage. The villain, the man who said yes at each turning point, was former prime minister Yasuhiro Nakasone.

After the LDP's smashing victory in the 1986 election, Nakasone suddenly and impulsively promised to provide the United States with military technology. Instead of using this asset to bargain for a quid pro quo—no trade sanctions, for example—he gave it away. Nakasone meant it as a great favor to the United States. He was about the only Japanese politician who understood the implications of the commitment, how much the Pentagon needed certain Japanese civilian technology with military applications. There was no outcry from either the LDP or opposition parties. Senior LDP leaders—Noboru Takeshita, Kiichi Miyazawa, and Shintaro Abe—did not grasp the significance of the premier's action. Our politicians still failed to comprehend the importance of Japan's amazing high technology, even though the Americans were beside themselves with fear. This lead in high technology is Japan's greatest strength, but for some reason we have not used it effectively in international politics. It is beyond my comprehension why, despite this fantastic advantage, Japanese prime ministers go to Washington and accede to every White House wish. That is my greatest complaint about Japan's foreign policy.

Nakasone's Great Failure

Nakasone gave away our technology; all he got in return was Reagan's friendship. You cannot lead a nation through perilous times with goodwill alone. Nakasone bragged about being on a first-name basis with President Reagan, and the media played up the "Ron-Yasu" connection. In fact, however, it was a one-way relationship. Nakasone was a yes-man to Reagan and betrayed our vital national interests. I recently asked a Reagan aide if Nakasone had ever disagreed sharply with or refused a request from the president. Grinning, he said he had never heard of it happening. Nakasone was a "wonderful person, a great friend" to the United States, he said.

Nakasone understood that Japan's high technology was superior to that of the United States and also that the Pentagon was desperately worried about reliance on Japanese microchips. Nevertheless, for his own reasons, he never said no to the United States. Was it because the U.S. government had something on him from the Lockheed bribery case in 1976? Or did it have incriminating or embarrassing information about another political scandal? Whatever the explanation, Nakasone did not press the advantage. I wish he had laid his cards on the table and had at least been tough enough to say, "My government takes a different view of the matter."

It was during Nakasone's watch that the next-generation

support fighter, code-named FSX (for fighter support experimental), designed by Mitsubishi Heavy Industries (MHI), became an issue between Tokyo and Washington. Nakasone caved in to U.S. pressure and agreed to codevelopment and production of the FSX. What secret deals took place I do not know, but I watched the process unfold with a heavy heart.

Mitsubishi Heavy Industries is typical of the first-rate, technology-driven companies in Japan. MHI's chief engineer is an extraordinary person. Working with a U.S. missile used by Japan's Self-Defense Forces (SDF), for example, he produced the best ground-to-air missile in the world. His thinking on the FSX was that the aircraft would be completely designed and manufactured in Japan. But when the Pentagon saw the FSX blueprints, it panicked. The design is fantastic. No other fighter around will be able to hold a candle to the MHI aircraft. It can easily shoot down the F-15 and F-16. Astounded at the prospect, U.S. Secretary of Defense Caspar Weinberger frantically tried to stop MHI from developing the FSX.

Unfortunately, Japan does not make jet engines. Ever since I was in the House of Councilors many years ago I have urged that we build them, but I have been ignored. For the FSX, we would have to buy F-15 and F-16 engines. If the United States refused to sell them, we could have purchased French models. France is one of those countries where the president preaches peace and the premier travels around the world peddling weapons. If Paris had declined the sale, we could have bought jet engines from Moscow, though they probably would not have been as good.

With U.S. engines, the FSX can attain 95 percent of the F-15 or F-16's speed. That slight loss of quickness is more than compensated for by its ability to turn in a tight radius, one-third the distance required by the F-15, F-16, and MiGs.

The U.S. fighters at maximum speed need 5,000 meters to make a complete turn; the FSX can do it in about 1,600 meters. The MHI fighter can get behind an enemy quickly, lock on to the target, and destroy it with a heat-seeking missile. The FSX has a vertical forward stabilizer located approximately beneath the pilot's seat. Shaped like a shark's fin, it enables the aircraft to change altitude, nose direction, pitch, and roll without changing its flight pattern. An analogy would be an automobile that can turn 360 degrees in either direction without moving forward or backward. It is a brilliant concept. American aeronautical engineers might have thought of it, too, but MHI was ready to build the aircraft.

To the Department of Defense, it was like a replay of the early stage of the Pacific War, when the Zero fighter dominated the skies. U.S. admirals had assumed the Imperial Navy had nothing to match their aircraft, but the Zero proved far superior. Now, Japan was building another menacing weapon.

The United States was determined to stop Japan from making the FSX. Perhaps, in discussions with Nakasone about the project, the Americans mentioned an old skeleton in the prime minister's closet. Whatever the reason, he capitulated, and MHI's wonderful FSX became a joint Japan-U.S. project. Later, in November 1988, officials of the Reagan and Takeshita administrations signed a memorandum of understanding on codevelopment. The principal contractors still had to agree on work shares, however, and General Dynamics Corporation tried to dictate the division of labor. At one point, its spokesman said that if the Japanese side disagreed with its proposal, the main wing could be divided into left and right components and built separately by U.S. and Japanese companies. It was one of many weird ideas from General Dynamics.

The crux of the FSX issue is that U.S. contractors want to steal Japanese know-how. Without our ceramics and carbon-filter resins, they cannot build a first-rate fighter. That is why the Pentagon pushed so hard for codevelopment. Some Japanese business leaders, perhaps overwhelmed by the U.S. offensive, say that though joint development is undesirable, we should go along with Washington on the FSX in the interest of the overall bilateral relationship. I disagree. Abandoning independent development of this aircraft is a terrible blunder. Under no circumstances should we go through with it.

If the U.S. cocontractors make unreasonable demands on the division of FSX work, Japan should withdraw from joint development. That would force the United States to deal with Japan's technical competence, our ability to build the plane independently. Japanese negotiators should say, "Codevelopment was decided by Nakasone and Reagan but there are new administrations in Tokyo and Washington now. We have reconsidered the project and have decided to build the FSX in Japan." Unless we jolt the Americans this way, they will push us around as usual. The country with the strong hand can raise the ante.

On a few occasions when I had a chance to talk to Nakasone, I mentioned the fighter project. "Oh, you followed the FSX issue? But of course you would," he said. "I compromised on the FSX to keep bilateral relations on an even keel," he told me. "When I was director-general of the Defense Agency back in 1970–71, the Americans were already alarmed at our fourth defense-buildup plan," he added. I could understand his behavior if it made the United States more respectful of Japan. But what he did was no compromise. It was a sellout.

The prime minister was in a position to say no to U.S. demands. We had the technological upper hand. His decision was utterly deplorable. Far from thanking Japan, Washington will only increase the blustering and arm-twisting. As Clayton

Yeutter has said, they believe pressure is the best tactic against Japan. Some Japanese, misinterpreting my position, have said, "You're trying to intimidate the United States. That's a very risky game. You'd better stop." But I am not the one making threats. Needless to say, it is particularly important that we establish an equal partnership with the United States at this time. That is why, if the circumstances warrant a firm rejection of a U.S. demand, Japan should unequivocally do so. Saying no is part of the bargaining process between equals. Acquiescent, compromise-prone diplomacy does not serve the national interest. Our technology makes us increasingly able to withstand pressure from Washington, but so far we have not maximized our advantage in the high stakes game of international politics. It is beyond me why, when our technology gives us leverage in certain key areas, our leaders do not act more confidently.

[. . .]

During a conversation with Glenn Fukushima, a Harvard-educated Japan specialist who is with the office of the U.S. Trade Representative, I asked him who he considered Japan's toughest negotiator. Without hesitation he named Makoto Kuroda, then vice-minister for international affairs, Ministry of International Trade and Industry (MITI). The Japanese media have depicted Kuroda as a hard-line troublemaker, and have said his outspoken comments in 1987 influenced the U.S. Congress to pass the retaliatory tariff on Japanese semiconductor products. The Americans have publicly called him obstinate, as well as other things, yet they respect him. If Kuroda considers a demand unreasonable, he refuses to budge. When a firm no is the correct response, he says it and keeps saying it. What distinguishes Kuroda from many Japanese officials is that he does not cave in to U.S. threats and become humbly deferential. The Americans, like the bully who thinks he can flex his muscles and intimidate a smaller opponent, keep pushing. Kuroda stands his ground and tells them to bash away. "You are the one who will regret it," he says, not flinching under the attack.

Kuroda is not a knee-jerk naysayer. He carefully explains the rationale behind Japan's decisions. This elucidation is the essence of negotiation. U.S. officials say, however, that nearly all Japanese politicians and bureaucrats make such vague and indirect statements that they cannot figure out Tokyo's stance. When the Americans react strongly to an unclear proposal, the Japanese side gets flustered and says yes to the U.S. position. But they do not really mean yes. They are just trying to smooth over an unpleasant confrontation. It is very unfortunate that our representatives have given the impression that Japan will not act without external pressure. This image of susceptibility to table-pounding and sanctions is detrimental to our diplomacy.

Half the staff in Japan's embassies should be from the private sector, not part of the career foreign service. Thousands of Japanese executives have crossed swords with their American or European counterparts in tough business dealings. Many would be effective advocates of Japan's interests. Akio Morita, for example, would make a splendid ambassador to Washington. Then we would see a change in Japan-U.S. relations.

CHAPTER 5

National Security and the Pacific Age

AN OPEN, direct confrontation with Washington on a major issue might have dramatic repercussions. The administration and Congress would be shocked, and the reverberations would spread across the United States, triggering strong reactions. Even my hypothetical comment about selling semiconductors to the Soviet Union provoked some Americans to say they would reoccupy Japan. Nevertheless, we should speak our minds and assert our national interests. Akio Morita has correctly noted that, for better or worse, the two countries cannot disengage from each other. Still, the United States is not the whole world for Japan. In a sense, for decades after World War II it was, but no longer. If the United States keeps harassing us, we should tell the Americans that Japan will define its role in a much broader framework. We have many options and may make a bold move.

[. . .]

Playing the Geopolitical Game

President Richard Nixon's rapprochement with China in 1972 is an interesting case study for Japan. According to my sources, the overture succeeded because of Chinese awe at U.S. high technology. The process began in 1971 when Henry Kissinger showed Mao Zedong and Zhou Enlai satellite photographs of Soviet forces along the Sino-Soviet border. I think Kissinger also showed them photos of the 1969 Ussuri River border clash. (I have seen these photographs.) The fighting began when a small Red Army detachment occupied Zhenbao Island and a much larger Chinese force drove it off. The Soviets committed more troops and seized the islands again. At that point, the Chinese escalated the fighting by deploying a full infantry division. The People's Liberation Army drove off the Soviet defenders, hoisted the Chinese flag, and celebrated their victory. Prematurely, as it turned out, because under the cover of a deep fog that enshrouded the island, the Soviets moved up a tank corps and opened fire on the massed Chinese infantry. When the fog lifted, Zhenbao was covered with piles of Chinese bodies. To complete the slaughter, Soviet tanks advanced against the Chinese infantry, eradicating all resistance. Kissinger apparently showed satellite coverage of the final operation to Beijing leaders. Convinced that they were virtually helpless militarily without high-tech reconnaissance and weapons systems, the Chinese kowtowed to Nixon and agreed to restore diplomatic relations. Washington played its technology card with great finesse.

In 1978, a border war erupted between Vietnam and China. Deng Xiaoping, who was in charge of military operations, foolishly started the conflict to teach the Vietnamese a lesson. The move backfired and Chinese forces were badly mauled, partly because of Moscow's support of Vietnam. Soviet spy satellites tracked Chinese forces and provided Hanoi with precise order of battle information—the number of troops leaving from Guangdong Station, movements of infantry divisions and tank units, battlefield deployments. Vietnam allowed Chinese forces to penetrate deep into the mountains and then attacked with antitank missiles, driving the Chinese units into a trap where they were destroyed.

U.S. spy satellites also monitored this inept Chinese offensive. Chiding Beijing's leaders for walking into an ambush, Carter administration officials showed them incredibly detailed satellite photos of the operation. (I have seen these photos, too.) The Chinese were again impressed at U.S. technical wizardry and this helped move the new relationship along.

Now the Americans are threatening to pull a similar end run with the Soviet Union. They say, in effect, "We can establish a close relationship with Moscow before you even realize what is going on, as we did with Beijing, and then we won't need Japan anymore." But if the United States can bluff this way, Japan can feint and parry, too.

Several senior members of the Japanese business community have been enthusiastic about developing Siberia since the early 1970s. The region's abundant natural resources are a powerful lure. Today, this idea seems very realistic. Some business leaders go so far as to say that if Moscow would return the four islands off Hokkaido that it has occupied since 1945, thereby clearing the way for a peace treaty, Japan would terminate the alliance with Washington and be neutral. Then Japan would get exclusive rights to develop Siberia. Japan has maglev, which the United States does not, and plenty of other high technology. So from a Soviet point of view, we ought to be the preferred partner.

Our opening move might be to encourage Soviet interest in a maglev high-speed system for Siberia. This would immediately run afoul of the COCOM ban on high-tech exports to Communist countries, but what is wrong with moving Siberia into the twenty-first century by drastically improving its rail system, shrinking the region's vast distances, and accelerating the movement of people and goods? We should be able to gain support from other countries and block U.S. efforts to stop the project. Britain and France skillfully maneuver this way all the time. Until Japan has leaders who understand Realpolitik, the United States will not regard us as an important player.

The "Free Ride" Myth

As the Occupation period was ending, the United States, concerned that Japan might again become a dangerous military power, assumed responsibility for our defense. But despite the claims of American spokesmen, the U.S. nuclear deterrent and U.S. bases here do not guarantee our security. I know this from personal experience and wrote about it twenty years ago. The U.S. nuclear umbrella is an illusion. As I have repeatedly warned, there is also no truth in the allegation, constantly and vociferously made by the U.S. Congress, that Japan is getting a free ride on defense. Japanese have believed the nuclear umbrella myth and the free-ride charges and were made to feel grateful and indebted to the United States.

Far from being the passive beneficiary of U.S. protection, Japan, thanks to its supremacy in high technology, was a primary factor in the arms limitation talks between Washington and Moscow. American security and foreign policy experts apparently foresaw that Japan's hammerlock on key technology would eventually force the superpowers to seek détente. Cognizant of Japan's potential, Kissinger often alluded to such an outcome. Unfortunately, Japanese politicians were too ignorant of military and technical matters to refute the nuclear umbrella myth and free-ride charges of congressional critics. On the other hand, U.S. leaders are reluctant to admit that Japan's technology is crucial to U.S. security.

The U.S. government is becoming seriously concerned about the consequences of technology-rich Japan aligning with another power. Some politicians and security officials have urged Japan to assume greater responsibility for regional defense—for example, sea-lanes up to 1,000 miles out into the Pacific—and such proposals warrant serious attention. However, whatever we finally decide about the alliance with the United States, we should reorganize our armed forces—presently constituted according to an inappropriate Pentagon strategic design—in line with our own priorities and make them a more efficient, high-tech deterrent. A would-be attacker must know that we will hit back hard and swiftly. That means heavy emphasis on tactics and strategy geared to repulsing an enemy.

Our navy is hardly suitable for that purpose. Japan has many escort vessels to participate in U.S.-controlled Pacific Rim exercises, the kind that would fire all their missiles in a minute or so and then be helpless. They contribute nothing to our security. In fact, U.S.-led joint naval exercises are irrelevant to our policy of exclusively defensive operations.

A top U.S. military officer admitted the inadequacy of present defense arrangements. Gen. Charles Dyke, former commander of the U.S. Army, Japan, told Ground Self-

Defense Force officer candidates that the probability of a Soviet invasion of Hokkaido, the main island closest to the U.S.S.R., was virtually nil.

Israel Tal, the former commander of Israel's tank forces, visited Japan and discomfited the Defense Agency by asking why Japan, a mountainous archipelago, was making tanks for the Self-Defense Forces. This great armor expert even questioned the point of deploying tank units in Hokkaido, with its relatively open spaces. Japan should destroy a Soviet invasion force at sea before it could land, Tal said. He also disputed the validity of equipping the Maritime SDF with frigates.

Tal is absolutely correct. All of this unsuitable equipment is the Pentagon's doing. By shaping Japan's armed forces according to a U.S. strategic plan, Washington was able to demonstrate its military might and that it would be a reliable ally.

Japan's flawed security policy is the result of four decades of acquiescent diplomacy. Our leaders have gone along with Washington on everything. It would be less expensive to defend ourselves than to continue the present arrangement with the United States. We have subordinated our security interests to America's global strategy and pay much of the cost of maintaining their forces in Japan. But that did not stop some members of Congress from claiming that U.S. naval operations during the Iran-Iraq War were "in defense of Japan at the cost of American blood."

If we are going to be blamed for American casualties in the Middle East, then this security arrangement is counterproductive. It is time a Japanese prime minister said, "We will protect ourselves with our own strength and wisdom." This will entail certain sacrifices. Although not yet politically feasible, with a popular consensus, we could do it. We have the technological and fiscal resources for an independent, defensive military force. I am not suggesting we abrogate the se-

curity treaty immediately. That is not realistic. Our
relationship with the United States is of fundamental importance and we owe much to the treaty. My point is that to rule
out this possibility—not even to think about it—deprives us of
an important bargaining chip. Today, the security treaty is no
longer indispensable. We have sufficient resources to maintain the present level of defense capability on our own.

Both the left and right in Japan become so emotional about
the security alliance that a reasoned national debate on the
issue has been impossible. Like it or not, however, before
long we will have to reassess the pact and make a decision.

The Liberal Democratic party as presently constituted will
not touch the question. Several changes would have to occur
in the political landscape. First, the opposition parties must
drop their pro-Soviet and pro-China positions. Next, they
must reach a par with the LDP in policy-making ability. That
would lead to a realignment of political forces—splits and
regroupings. Then, if the public supported the new lineup,
Japan would have greater flexibility on security.

Regional Prosperity

Japanese popular songs are sung throughout East and Southeast Asia, a phenomenon similar to the impact of American
pop music on Japan after World War II. We hummed the Top
Ten tunes, became fascinated with the American way of life,
and created a U.S.-style mass-consumption society.

What is the source of Japan's new dynamism? On the sur-
face, it is our high-tech culture and life-style. The mainspring,
of course, is our industrial technology, in which we are ahead
even of the Americans. Technological breakthroughs have always been the agent of change, whether in the Stone, Bronze,

or Computer ages. Technology gives rise to civilization, upon which, in time, culture thrives. Nations decline when they self-indulgently let life-styles become more important than workmanship and neglect their industrial and technological base. That is the lesson of history.

Japan, not the West, triumphed in semiconductors—new microchips and defect-free manufacturing—because of our ability to refine things. When the late André Malraux, France's minister of culture, saw the wooden statue of the future Buddha at the Koryuji temple in Kyoto, he said it symbolized an eternal sublimity transcending race and religion, the majesty of a supreme being or Buddha. By contrast, he said, Rodríguez de Silva Velázquez's painting of "Christ on the Cross" and similar realistic Western religious art have a grotesque, even disgusting quality that might alienate the faithful. All who gaze upon this statue bow their heads and join their hands in solemn supplication. You feel the presence of a divine spiritual force. The statue exemplifies the extraordinary Japanese gift for enhancing Buddhist aesthetics that originated in India and reached these shores via China and Korea. One might say we have added a finishing touch to the great East Asian tradition.

We owe this talent to our geographic location as an island cul de sac off the continent of Asia, the final stopping point of the religious and intellectual movements that spread across the mainland in ancient times. Energy that might have gone, for example, into transmitting the glory of Buddhist art to other lands turned inward. An accident of geography made us adept at refining, embellishing, and improving.

Minoru Genda, a former chief of staff of the Air SDF, a member of the House of Councilors, and an authority on military lore, has noted the effect of this talent on weapons. In the West, the sport of fencing evolved from warfare, but the foil, épée, and saber never became more than fancy kitchen

knives, mere tools for killing people. Japanese swords, however, are works of art. Crafted here by master smiths for more
than a millennium, our swords have superb texture, elegance,
and balance. Viewing these blades, even non-Japanese sense
the mystery of perfection. We refined a lethal weapon into an
aesthetic experience.

Genda once said to me, "Japan will be all right. We can
defend ourselves." When I asked him what he meant, he said,
"With our technology." His idea was that our national gift for
improving and refining everything from Buddhist art to semiconductors is the keystone of our security. I agreed completely, adding that we must press ahead and develop new
technology with diverse potential applications, without becoming a major military power. Genda said Japan should gain
a five-year lead in certain major technologies and try to extend it to a full decade. With a ten-year advantage, Japan
would be secure through 2025. The question remains, however, whether Japanese politicians can use our high-tech card
effectively in the international arena.

In a recent discussion with an American journalist, I ex-
pounded at length on how the white man, especially Americans, had not carried his burden well. I pointed out that the
developing countries in regions that had been under Caucasian control, or where the West was still giving aid and advice, were a mess. Look at Africa, Central and South America,
the Middle East. The only basket case in Asia is a country the
United States ruled, the Philippines. Americans have the incredible illusion that the Philippines is a showcase of democracy, which shows there is something basically wrong with
their perception. Good intentions have produced very bad
results.

I told the journalist that U.S. rule was more benevolent
than that of the Spanish, so Filipinos are friendly and accom-

modating to the Americans. Nevertheless, the United States never taught them real democracy. Congressman Stephen J. Solarz, chairman of the House Subcommittee on Asian and Pacific Affairs, once sounded me out on helping Manila. The Aquino government had requested a huge amount of foreign aid, [part of which could be used to compensate wealthy landowners whose estates would be confiscated in a land reform]. Perhaps Washington and Tokyo could each provide half, he said. What a joke! [I am underwhelmed by a person who wants to pour money into a country with such a great gap between the rich and poor and where the lower ranks of the bureaucracy are still just as corrupt as during the Marcos regime.] Only a person who knew nothing about conditions in the Philippines would think that just giving them money would turn the country around. Solarz did not understand where those funds would end up. Filipinos have to resolve their own social contradictions. Outsiders pouring in money will not cure anything.

To help the Philippines, first the malefactors have to be identified: the landowners. This class, with its vast holdings and absurd privileges, plundered wealth from the people. I have no sympathy with this exploitative elite. Unless a far-reaching land reform like the one in Japan after World War II is carried out, rural desperation will spawn radical, violent agrarian movements. Without the stability of social justice and a middle class, the landlords, too, will be insecure. If the military take power and adopt leftist policies—confiscation, nationalization—that will be the end of the big landowners.

First remove the exploiters, and then democracy can take root. The U.S. "showcase of democracy" is all show and no substance. Not only would it be a waste of money to spend billions of dollars to compensate landlords for their estates, but it would destroy Filipino self-reliance, their ability to solve their own problems. With nations or individuals, self-help—the determination to pull oneself up by the bootstraps—is crucial. Unaware of what makes other people tick, Americans, perhaps because of their naïveté, think giving money will ensure happiness.

I told the American journalist about the chieftain on Truk who lamented the difference between Japanese and American rule in Micronesia. In fluent Japanese, he said to me that his children had only learned sloth and laziness from the Americans. U.S. rulers had spoiled the younger generation on Belau, Truk, and throughout Micronesia with money and materialism. Lettuce, for example, can be grown on the islands, but instead of agronomy, U.S. administrators taught the Micronesians how to import it.

Americans have no respect for the local culture, the chief said. Their missionaries disapproved of tribal medicine men and prohibited the use of medicinal herbs and folk remedies. The natives were not allowed to use cures for burns and cuts that were often more effective than modern pharmaceuticals. The traditional songs and dances were dying out, the chief said, because the missionaries had also banned local festivals. Like barbarians, the Americans destroy the local people's culture, impose their own, and do not even realize what they have done.

In the old days, the islanders held a harvest festival similar to autumn celebrations in Japan. In fact, people from the South Seas may have taught them to our ancestors. Villagers gathered under the full moon and danced to the beat of drums. Young people paired off, of course. Rural festivals always have a ribald, licentious side. The missionaries banned this raucous, earthy celebration and made the harvest festival a tribute to God. Villagers placed food offerings on the church altar, which the minister and his family later ate! We didn't grow the food for them, the chieftain explained. The missionaries were unaware of how their piety was misinterpreted.

I concluded my little lecture to the journalist by pointing out that the Asian countries that are booming economically—South Korea, Taiwan, Singapore, etc.—were all controlled by Japan at one time before or during World War II. Admittedly, Japan behaved badly during the conflict and soul searching is in order, but in some ways we were also a beneficial influence. Of the resource-supplying regions, Southeast Asia is the only one where, thanks to intensive effort, including Japan's contribution, the countries are making rapid social and economic progress. You cannot say that about any place where Caucasians were preeminent. The journalist had no comeback.

The miracle of Asia, symbolized by the emergence of the Four Tigers (South Korea, Taiwan, Hong Kong, and Singapore), is a wonderful development. Rather than fear these newly industrialized economies (NIEs), Japan should be a force for regional prosperity. By tactful, sensitive help and leadership, we must be part of Asia's future. As the Age of the Pacific dawns, the region will be even more vital to Japan's maturity than the United States.

Joining the World Community

To take our place in the global community, we must be neither subservient nor throw our weight around like a superpower. We need just the right amount of self-confidence, as individuals and a nation. Many Japanese see Japan as separate from the rest of the world, as if we were on parallel lines that never meet rather than inside concentric circles. This view stems in part from linguistic and cultural isolation but, more important, from geopolitical factors. We must discard this typically Japanese way of looking at the outside world.

How do we, the outsiders, join the community of nations? Not the Nakasone way—the famed Ron-Yasu relationship, with Nakasone insinuating himself next to the U.S. president at the summit meetings of the seven industrial democracies. The principled way is to say no to Washington on a matter like the FSX. An act of reasoned, dignified independence will change popular Japanese perceptions of the world. It is a kind of rite of passage that would mark our maturity as a nation and our equality with the United States. Both are prerequisites for full-fledged membership in the world community. By dropping the role of yes-men, we would win the respect of other nations—China, for one.

Japan and the United States should constitute a Group of Two that works to solve global issues. An equal partnership would help confirm Japan's status in the world, and I think Washington would see the advantages. In such a relationship, Japan would frequently have to disagree, after carefully explaining our reasons. The Japanese government would also have to reject the special pleading of domestic special interest groups clamoring for protectionism.

Today, the worldwide attention focused on Japan is due to our prosperity and wealth. Of course, money counts, but we also have tradition and culture, wellsprings of creativity, and high technology neither Moscow nor Washington can ignore. To be fully appreciated, we must, when matters of crucial national interest warrant, articulate our position and say no to the United States.

Part Two

CHAPTER 6

Japan and the United States: Partners or Master and Servant?

EVEN I, who respect American ideals of loyalty and fairness—
in fact, precisely because I esteem these values—cannot accept many actions Washington takes. Again, the U.S.
turnabout on the FSX is one.

Certain political issues are a watershed. The choices a country's leaders make profoundly affect popular consciousness
and the society's direction. Sometimes nations are unaware
that a course of action has epoch-making significance and realize it only in hindsight. The FSX dispute is such a case, and

I cannot help wondering what on earth Tokyo and Washington were thinking. Should a matter involving one country's security and so vital to its future be handled so carelessly?

Few Americans or Japanese realize the implications of the FSX controversy. One congressman justified the U.S. demand for codevelopment on the grounds of Japan's trade surplus with the United States, but that is farfetched. Washington forced us to submit on the FSX; Japan had to accept one-sided demands. Yet there was no reaction among the public in either country. That is another reason why the FSX affair symbolizes the relationship between the two nations: both peoples take such unequal arrangements for granted.

The FSX mystery involves the unprecedented renegotiation of an official memorandum of understanding (MOU) signed by Reagan and Takeshita administration officials in November 1988. The Bush administration insisted on "clarifying" key provisions of the memorandum and reopened talks. The U.S. attitude was appalling; Japan's weak-kneed posture was even worse. We should have said, "No, a deal is a deal," and flatly refused to discuss the MOU. Instead, we ignobly acceded to U.S. pressure. I want to review the FSX saga to show how utterly unfair it was.

The fighter support experimental (FSX) is tailored to Japan's war-renouncing Constitution. Its combat mission is to intercept hostile aircraft, ships, or troops entering Japanese territory and provide tactical ground support for friendly forces. The word "support" means that, unlike attack fighters, the FSX cannot strike directly at targets in enemy territory. Air Self-Defense Force (ASDF) pilots must operate only in our air space; they cannot extend the fighting to the enemy's homeland.

Several years ago, the Japan Socialist party (JSP) made an

issue of U.S. Phantom fighters purchased by the Defense Agency, claiming that the aircraft had an offensive capability incompatible with the Constitution. In the end, the bombing mechanism had to be removed from the ASDF planes.

The FSX was conceived to meet Japan's topography and peculiar constitutional constraints: It is an exclusively defensive aircraft that can engage and destroy attacking planes over this narrow archipelago. These special requirements led to the government-industry consensus on producing it domestically instead of purchasing a U.S. aircraft.

The F-15Js made in Japan under a licensing agreement had fewer mechanical failures and accidents than those purchased from the U.S. maker. A jet trainer developed in Japan was completed in 1985 on schedule, and without cost overruns, a sign of our aerodynamic competence. Thus, civilian and military engineers were confident of their two-engine FSX design and dropped the single-engine F-16 from consideration.

Nevertheless, U.S. pressure turned the FSX into a joint development of an improved model of the F-16. Defense Agency and MHI officials felt betrayed by the decision. I met with MHI president Yotaro Iida and vice-president Takaaki Yamada to ascertain the facts of this matter. In the course of our conversation, I compared the FSX deal to an arranged marriage. "We were expecting a virgin of twenty-one but what we got was a divorcée in her thirties," I said. "That's going a bit too far," Yamada corrected. "Let's say in her late twenties."

Why do we have to accept a shotgun wedding? The problem, as I have said before, is partly the unwillingness of Japanese officials to stand up to Washington. They believe deference, even to the point of servility, is safer than confrontation. This pervasive attitude stems from our defeat in World War II. To call this stance a foreign policy would be a misnomer; it is the acceptance of the subordinate status of a tributary state.

The FSX is a crucial multibillion-dollar project involving Japan's air defenses into the twenty-first century. Craven capitulation to Washington on such an issue showed the world that the best way to treat Japan is with force majeure. And the more absurd your case, the harder you should press it.

Early in the Pacific War, the Zero fighter dominated the skies, much to the amazement of the U.S. Navy. Given the very different world we live in today, I do not like to think that the Americans are haunted by the past. Nevertheless, although Japan is now a friendly country, our ability to produce a new Zero may have triggered a kind of delayed stress-reaction syndrome. This would explain why, even before the Commerce Department and Congress got involved, the Pentagon sounded a different warning about the FSX.

In 1987, a group of Pentagon aeronautics experts visited Japan on a fact-finding mission. Until then, the U.S. position was that a Japanese FSX would be economically and technically unfeasible. The team drastically revised this view, warning that Japan's aviation industry could some day threaten U.S. aerospace hegemony. From that point, trade and commercial spinoffs were linked to the security question, and the pressure resulted in joint development. Obviously, Japan did not want this arrangement.

Codevelopment clearly favored American interests. Yet in January 1989, Clyde V. Prestowitz, Jr., a former Commerce Department official, published a lengthy attack on codevelopment in *The Washington Post*. It will "give Japan a big boost toward its long-sought goal: leadership in air-craft manufacture, one of the last areas of American high-technology dominance," he wrote. Japan should buy "50 F-16s or F-18s immediately, either off the shelf or with relatively minor modifications." And U.S. companies should have a 50 percent work share in both development and production. Whatever his objective, the article was an irrational diatribe. Prestowitz wanted Japan to buy a fighter that we know will be obsolete in a few years! And we would be the only country purchasing the F-16. Is the United States serious about Japan's defense? Prestowitz, who instigated the opposition to joint development, seems to be the standard-bearer for American technonationalism. Japan had conceded, but then Washington pushed even further, trying to get every advantage. It was frightening to see how ruthless Americans can be.

The "clarifications" incorporated in April 1989 as side letters to the original MOU place strict limits on the transfer of F-16 technology. Japan must obtain U.S. approval in order to use it for other purposes or transfer it to another country. The "clarifications" state explicitly that in principle Japan cannot use the technology for other purposes. However, there are no similar written provisions regarding the high technology we provide the United States, only spoken assurances. Furthermore, Japan must turn over all new technology generated by codevelopment. U.S. demands on technological breakthroughs are stipulated in writing; Japan's are only a spoken understanding.

Here are the major unfair aspects of joint development:

1. Japan transfers technology free.
2. Japan pays patent and licensing fees for U.S. technology.
3. The United States restricts technology transfers, including the refusal to provide vital software, the source codes that govern flight control, and electronic warfare systems.

4. Japan is prohibited from diverting technology to civilian applications.
5. General Dynamics is guaranteed more than a 40 percent work share.

This is a classic one-sided agreement. The Bush administration was able to drive this hard bargain because Japan was preoccupied with the Recruit stocks-for-favors scandal, and Diet members are uninformed about defense matters. The government was, as usual, pusillanimous. It is disgraceful that Japan's political parties could not put aside their squabbling over the Recruit briberies and hold a bipartisan debate to block this demeaning agreement. The work share provision, especially, poses a major problem for Japanese auditors. If the opposition parties had looked into these terms, the Diet probably would have insisted on making revisions in the budget bill.

National security is the issue that will help Japanese cast off their subservient attitude toward the United States, along with certain Occupation-inspired changes. The FSX is a splendid example of what is wrong between Tokyo and Washington. We should not compromise. Building an indigenous, superior support fighter, even if it costs more than F-16s off the shelf, might finally remove the ambiguity in the U.S.-inspired Constitution. Are we allowed to defend ourselves with our own military forces? A made-in-Japan FSX would end guilt feelings that the SDF violated the Constitution.

Regarding nuclear weapons, Charles De Gaulle said that a great country like France could not entrust its fate to other nations. Although the atomic arms had no strategic significance, France acquired them, successive governments modernized the *force de frappe*, and NATO members accepted France's possession of an independent nuclear deterrent. By comparison, developing an indigenous FSX is a much more meaningful project. Another hard look at codevelopment is in our own national interest and would contribute to a new relationship with the United States.

Rethinking Japan's Defense

Japan's security system was flawed from the start. The Self-Defense Forces grew out of the National Police Reserve (NPR), which the U.S. Occupation (1945–52) created in 1950 following the outbreak of the Korean War. The SDF was a miniature version of America's armed forces, but our defense budget, reflecting Japan's small gross national product (GNP), was minuscule compared to U.S. military outlays. As Japan's GNP increased, so did the SDF, but except for not having nuclear weapons, it remains a carbon copy of the U.S. military.

After World War II, the United States appointed itself policeman for the free world and intervened militarily in Europe, Asia, and the Middle East. Japan can fight only if attacked, and then only on home ground. Our defense posture is qualitatively different, and weaponry and combat capability should reflect that fact. The FSX's armaments, for example, should be different from those on an F-16.

Why do we keep a large, expensive tank force in Hokkaido, which has so much mountainous terrain? Why does the MSDF need large frigates? The tanks are there on the assumption that enemy armored units will establish a beachhead and then push inland. Assuming that scenario, what the MSDF needs to stop the attackers in the water is not frigates but high-speed, missile-equipped vessels. They would be more effective and less expensive. As I mentioned earlier, a top U.S. military officer has implicitly admitted the inadequacy of present defense arrangements. But when Gen. Charles Dyke, former commander of the U.S. Army, Japan, told Ground Self-Defense Force officer candidates that the probability of a Soviet invasion of Hokkaido was virtually nil, he believed that the SDF and the U.S.-Japan Mutual Security Treaty are largely responsible for that.

Japan's military forces are merely an auxiliary to U.S. global strategy. Their function is to supplement U.S. power in East Asia; protecting Japan is a by-product. While most Japanese have regarded military matters as taboo and ignored national security, our defense structure has become a house of cards, riddled with the jokers of false assumptions.

No matter how many billions of dollars we spend trying to have all kinds of weapons and make the three services happy, our defense structure will be inadequate. For example, the command centers that control our early-warning radar and the fighter squadrons that are Japan's first line of defense have not been placed in hardened underground sites. They are exposed, sitting ducks for an enemy attack, as we buy more tanks and warships. Japan is so vulnerable because our defenses were built in accordance with Washington's wishes, not our own priorities. We need new weapons suited to our special situation; to get them, we should cut the fat from the military budget.

Our basic strategic assumptions are wrong. Every year the United States insists that Japan "do more on defense" and accept greater "burden sharing." We increase the military budget yearly—it's now a sacred cow with a voracious appetite for tax dollars—and the U.S. Congress still criticizes us for not spending enough. Ironically, flawed premises make this money a huge investment in futility. By streamlining the armed forces, we could reduce the burden on the taxpayers and upgrade our defense capability.

I am not proposing indigenous weapons just for the sake of national pride or saying that all SDF weapons must be made in Japan. The FSX is a priceless opportunity to come to grips with the issue of defense spending, which has been semi-taboo, and to reevaluate the Japan–U.S. partnership, including our subservient mentality.

We have to do this by our own lights, not in the context of U.S. strategy. The usual pro-American tilt would be counterproductive. The Americans will look out for their own national interests: It is up to us to protect Japan. What our own forces cannot do, we will ask the United States to help us with.

A few years ago, in a burst of *glasnost*, Moscow invited the Defense Agency and Japanese journalists to observe their Pacific Fleet's maneuvers in the Japan Sea. The United States was upset for some reason and through the Foreign Ministry tried to block Japanese participation.

The Defense Agency regarded it as a rare opportunity to see the Soviet navy close up and wanted to go. But the Foreign Ministry, the enthusiastic intermediary for Washington, undercut the Agency, which had to decline the invitation. Ironically, Japanese journalists went, so only the military professionals were denied a firsthand look at Soviet naval strength. The U.S. clearly interfered in Japan's national interests.

Later, Toshitsugu Taoka, who covered the story for the *Asahi Shimbun*, said, "In many respects the Soviet navy lags far behind the West. Their warships are incredibly inferior in quality and equipment to those of the United States and Japan. The Americans probably did not want Japanese defense officials to see that for themselves, out of fear that Japan would downgrade the Soviet military threat. Japanese would feel less obligated to Washington and psychologically more inclined to go our own way on defense."

Taoka's conclusions ring true. The way U.S. officials handle Japan reminds me of the proverb said to have been the political philosophy of Ieyasu Tokugawa, founder of the Tokugawa shogunate : "Keep the people dependent and ignorant." The Pentagon may even have thought that if Japanese were aware of its overwhelming naval superiority, we might, as Washington's major creditor, have suggested cuts in the navy's budget to reduce the federal deficit. Perhaps the real reason is that the American people are unaware that the Soviets are no match for the U.S. Navy, and the admirals do not want them to find out from Japanese reports. When I think that the Foreign Ministry was a lackey for the Pentagon on this, I do not know whether to laugh or cry.

Is not Japan a U.S. puppet? At least on military matters, that is exactly what we are. Unable to rein in Japan's economic and technological dynamism, Washington is determined come what may to control our defense policy.

Japanese are well aware that the United States has been our friend and protector since World War II. Nevertheless, the claim, frequently heard on Capitol Hill, that the United States is still defending us sounds hollow today. Few Defense Agency officials would accept it. Granted, the mutual security treaty remains the bedrock of our national defense, but the specific arrangements, first elaborated in the early postwar years, should be drastically changed.

The numerous U.S. bases in Japan enable Washington to project military power from the West Coast to Capetown. They are more important to U.S. global strategy than to the defense of Japan. Any senior U.S. military officer will admit this; it is stated in Department of Defense reports. Thus it is very strange indeed that our military budget includes a multibillion-dollar category to pay much of the cost of keeping U.S. forces here. From the standpoint of which country benefits from the bases, Japan would be well justified in collecting user fees. That is essentially West Germany's position on U.S. bases, though Bonn does not charge a fee. The base issue is another reason why a review of national security deserves top priority.

Often, when I comment on defense matters, my critics at home and abroad call me a "neonationalist," "right-winger," an "irredentist" who wants to revive the "Greater East Asia Coprosperity Sphere," or an "apologist for the aggression of the 1930s." The charges only prove what closed little minds such people have. To label someone a menace for thinking about his country's security shows bias or arrogance.

Does the United States Regard Japan as an Equal Partner?

When most Japanese say, "The United States is an indispensable partner for Japan," they are expressing admiration and respect for America. But I often have the feeling that when Americans call on Japan to be an "equal partner," they really think that we are inferior, still unworthy of their admiration and respect.

Why do the two peoples have such different feelings about each other? One reason is the legacy of the Pacific War, the victors or losers mentality. Another is that Americans still have a superpower mindset. You can see flashes of this in James Fallows's article "Containing Japan" in *The Atlantic Monthly* of May 1989. Fallows writes: "Unless Japan is contained, therefore, several things that matter to America will be jeopardized: America's own authority to carry out its foreign policy and advance its ideals." He regrets the "sense that the United States is so deep in debt that it can't afford to do many of the things a leading power should do—explore space, improve its schools, maintain its military bases in Japan so that Japan doesn't build its own army, and so on." The comment about U.S. bases shows the U.S.'s motives, I think, namely that the real purpose of U.S. forces in Japan is to keep an eye on our military.

Americans like Fallows consider their "ideals" absolute values, a self-righteousness that blinds them to how annoying their "authority" to "advance" them often is to other countries. Fallows concludes by saying, "We do have the right to defend our interests and our values, and they are not identical to Japan's."

Fallows is correct that the two countries do not share identical interests and values. Yet we do not have to see the world exactly the same way to be partners. We can agree to disagree about many things. Equality is not homogeneity. That is the fallacy in Fallows's argument. He wants to "contain" the Japanese people because we are different. Japan and the United States would want to preserve their own interests and values whether they were allies or not. We have a partnership and should grant each other some leeway. Without nationalism— a strong sense of roots and identity—there cannot be internationalism, only a shallow cosmopolitanism. A country that always says yes to its ally is a vassal state, not an equal.

An American politician whom I know well said to me, "The Japan-U.S. relationship must be preserved. As you say, it's important to both countries and to the rest of the world. We're married to each other." "Well, if we are properly married, okay," I responded. "A wife can talk back to her husband. But a kept woman, afraid the man will kick her out, always has to do what he says. Don't ever think Japan is America's mistress." He was shocked at my metaphor, but we both laughed.

Today, many Americans overreact if Japan has the temerity to act like an independent nation. This happened with the FSX. Using their standard technique of fabricated charges, congressmen attacked the Mitsubishi Group as a way of getting at MHI. They claimed that Mitsubishi was helping Libya to build a chemical plant to produce poison gas. Later, the allegations were shown to be completely false. Undeterred by truth, these august legislators then demanded that Japan pledge not to help the Libyans build the facility in the future! It was as if a person accused of theft was shown to be innocent, and then the accusers, instead of apologizing, demanded that he promise never to steal again. This is the country that professes to treat Japan as an equal.

Americans will say, "Ishihara, you are the one with a belligerent, uncooperative attitude. You said Japan could change the military balance by selling semiconductors to the Soviet Union and cutting off the United States." It was a very provocative statement, I admit, but I had good reason to say it. This is what happened.

I was in Washington in 1987, right after Congress passed the resolution on semiconductors. I was at a reception where members of Congress and lobbyists for the U.S. semiconductor industry were gloating over their victory. There were remarks like "We got them this time," and "This'll knock the Japanese back a bit." Antipathy to Japan was as thick as an oil spill. Several congressmen made very intemperate comments to me. One said, "Profound changes are under way in the world that may fundamentally alter the U.S.-Japan relationship." I had heard the same kind of remark in Tokyo, so it was not news, but I pretended not to understand and asked what he meant.

"U.S.-Soviet ties have dramatically improved and it's quite possible that the partnership between Washington and Tokyo might be dissolved," he said gravely. "The United States may even abandon Japan." Laughingly I replied, "Do you mean that Americans and Russians have rediscovered their mutual identity as Caucasians?" He nodded in agreement. I went on, "I will never be a great fan of the Soviet Union, but if the United States no longer wants Japan as an ally, then we will have a free hand to look for other friends around the world. By the same token, in this new situation, when Moscow shops for high technology, it has a choice between Japan and the United States. If Japan sells certain semiconductors to the Soviet Union, which only we produce in quantity, wouldn't the United States be in deep trouble?"

Suddenly the mood became very tense. Our congressional host intervened, "It is premature to say that the Soviet-U.S. confrontation is over."

Despite the temporary awkwardness, I made some friends there, people with whom I could speak frankly. One reason I have always respected Americans is that most of them would not break off a personal relationship just because of a heated exchange.

But I could not get over that congressman's nod of assent when I asked if the Russo-American détente was based on both being white. It is perfectly all right for Americans and Russians to be friendly, of course. But if that means the end of the Japan-U.S. relationship, what have we been doing for the last forty years?

That congressman would not have said to a German or French politician, "We may even abandon you." Even if the comment was a childish threat inspired by frustration over trade imbalances, behind it was prejudice against nonwhite races. Americans get very upset when I tell them that Caucasians are biased against nonwhites. All human beings have feelings or attitudes they prefer not to talk about. Bringing up the race problem may violate an American taboo, but I take the risk because it affects whether the partnership between our countries is equal. Of course, I'm not suggesting Japanese are without fault. Discrimination is still widespread in Japan. I think Americans and Japanese should admit the obvious.

A Japanese businessman told me of an incident that happened to him and his wife in the United States. One night they went into a restaurant that was virtually empty. A waiter rudely said, "We're full," and turned them away. The executive admires the United States and knows the country well. Unlike me, he is tactful and does not complain about racial prejudice there. Despite this experience, he speaks highly of American society. He adds, however, that it would be an even greater country if it were not for the hostility toward nonwhites.

Perhaps because I have brought up race and been consistently outspoken about other matters that needed airing, an American congressman once said, "You're very direct and provocative for a Japanese. What makes you this way?"

I replied joking, "As a teenager I was struck for no reason by an American soldier."

I told him the whole story. It happened in 1946 when I was a second-year middle-school student. I lived in Zushi, then a quiet seaside resort of about 15,000 people, an hour south of Tokyo by train. Many U.S. troops were stationed in the area because there were former Imperial Navy ammunition dumps nearby.

One day in late August I was walking along the main business street on my way home from school. Three young GIs eating water ices approached from the opposite direction. The war had only been over a year and Japanese in Zushi still timidly moved aside for Americans. The new rulers had the street to themselves and that swaggering trio seemed to glory

in the deference. I did not like their attitude, so I walked
straight ahead, pretending not to see them. Just as I was
about to pass, one GI hit me in the face with his water ice. I
guess he did not like my attitude either. I ignored him and
continued walking. Other Japanese were watching me, fearful
of an incident. I remember feeling proud.

The congressman looked very embarrassed. I felt he was
taking it too seriously, so I said, "It's a true story but I meant
it as a humorous explanation of my outspokenness. Don't
make too much of it. That was a long time ago. It didn't make
me anti-American. Later I was crazy about U.S. pop music."

"But you'll never forget it."

"I guess I won't," I replied.

A bit later in the evening, he came up to me. "About your
story, were those GIs black?"

Bemused by the question, I said, "No, two were blond and
one was a redhead. They still had freckles on their faces."

The congressman, out of friendly concern for what the incident might have meant to me, had inadvertently revealed
his own prejudice.

I do not recount this exchange to make fun of racial prejudice among white Americans. There is a certain historical
justification for Caucasian attitudes toward other races. Europeans created most of the modern era and they feel superior
to Africans and Orientals, who were unable to modernize
rapidly and became colonies. Although the Japanese were the
only nonwhite people to avoid Western domination, it is not
surprising that Europeans and Americans look down on us,
too. But as we enter a new era in which Japan and the United
States will be the leading players, that attitude imperils trust
and cooperation. My point is that Americans ought to face
their prejudice toward Japan and overcome it.

Underlying Caucasian racial prejudice is their intense class consciousness, a bias against people of the same race or ethnic group but of different social strata. The European nobility despised commoners and the lower social orders just because they were not of their privileged level, while the hoi polloi both hated the nobility and aspired to their prestige and social standing. Eventually, a democratic fiction that everyone is created equal obscured the obvious hostility between the upper, middle, and lower classes. The nobility prided themselves on a life of ease. Gentlemen did not go into commerce, much less work with their hands. Disregarding the fact that they also benefited from the toil of the masses, the aristocracy viewed the other classes with contempt simply because they worked.

This class consciousness has persisted into the modern era. Western societies still have extraordinary disparities between strata and there is ubiquitous discrimination against the working class. In the United States, for example, fast-track members of the corporate elite will not even type a letter or do secretarial tasks for themselves. To go into the factory and get dirty and sweaty learning how products are made is beneath them.

Class background largely determines the quality of education an American receives. Highly trained U.S. top management do not ask blue-collar personnel for suggestions about how to improve factory operations. Even if they did, the workers probably would have little to say. The situation is quite different in Japan, as the example of the young NEC female employee mentioned earlier illustrates. She used her knowledge and training to discover the cause of defects in semiconductors. In any case, few countries have as egalitarian a class structure as Japan. Lech Walesa, former chairman of Solidarity, visited Japan and toured several factories. After seeing the easy interaction of blue-collar workers, supervisors, and executives, he remarked that Japan was the ideal socialist country. It was a heartfelt and accurate observation, I think.

In Japan, there is no open discrimination on the basis of position, class (everyone knows the word but the postwar generation has no feeling for what it really means), or income. In Europe and the United States, such discrimination is taken for granted. The people I meet in the West are all members of some elite—politics, business, journalism—and when I raise this issue, they do not take it seriously.

Class distinctions reflect the influence of the Catholic Church on Western civilization. Catholic thought celebrated the spirit or intellect and denigrated the body. Consequently, the clergy and nobility disdained labor, especially physical or manual forms, which symbolized the flesh. Although this elite could not have survived without the labor of ordinary people and certainly had their share of carnal desires, an artificial division of society into classes justified their superiority.

Lee Iacocca, chairman of Chrysler Corporation and a cheerleader of the Japan-bashers with his speeches and TV commercials, typifies that irresponsible breed of American executives who have become fabulously wealthy on the backs of American workers. Instead of being castigated for his price-gouging methods and huge bonuses, he is a kind of folk hero and was even mentioned as a presidential candidate. Iacocca's popularity is not so much incredible as absurd. I agree with Akio Morita's scathing comments about highly paid American executives. Japanese consumers are often said to be naive, and that is true in spades of American workers.

Certain groups in Japan have, in the past, also suffered discrimination for historical or political reasons. But ubiquitous discrimination remains a fixture of Western societies. Class-conscious and racist attitudes are deeply entrenched in the Caucasian psyche. No matter how much nonwhites object, Westerners will not soon shed their prejudices.

History gives nations periods of preeminence and decline. These temporary fluctuations in fortunes should not be permanent barriers between people. As a popular Japanese song goes, while you're still crying about one scene, the next has begun. Time marches on.

If the attitude in the United States is that people do not want to hear about all this from a Japanese, then they are hopeless. I believe our partnership will largely shape the next stage of human history. But if Americans say, "Who invited Japan to the party?" then we face a strife-ridden future.

CHAPTER 7

Americans: Look in the Mirror!

I REALIZE that these are very trying times for Americans. Until very recently, the United States was the unrivaled military and economic leader of the free world. Now, suddenly, Japan seems to have usurped that economic power. Americans from all walks of life are upset, frustrated, and worried about their country.

Most of America's woes are self-made, but some prefer to blame Japan, saying that our market is closed to U.S.-made products and we are an unfair trader. Those who cannot take stock of themselves—whether an individual, company, or nation—face an uncertain future. I want to believe that the United States, with its enormous underlying strength, will pull itself together and come roaring back. Yet there are many worrisome signs.

In October 1989, *Newsweek* reported that most Americans viewed Japan as a greater threat than the Soviet Union. The word "threat" might be appropriate if Americans had attempted to put their house in order. Instead, Congress looks to Japan for a scapegoat, uses high-handed tactics, and tries to push us around. To confuse a hypothetical military foe with an economic competitor and stick a ridiculous label like "threat" on us shows how dangerously confused the United States is. It would be fairer and more productive if Americans stopped the arm-twisting and sanctions and got their country back into shape.

Japan can help by compromise and cooperation, but the outcome depends primarily on American efforts. Let's be candid. America's problem is not Japan's economic strength but its own industrial weakness. As many senior Japanese executives have pointed out, the fundamental cause is the endemic shortsightedness in U.S. boardrooms. Some uninformed Americans make long lists of the evils of Japanese-style management and demand corrective action. Of course, there are impediments to free trade in Japan, but our businessmen are always ready to make reasonable adjustments. Before pointing the finger at Tokyo and Osaka, Americans should deal first with the host of problems in their own backyard.

A Japanese friend of mine established his own company and built it into a medium-sized corporation with a U.S. subsidiary. He is convinced that the complete separation of capital and management in the United States hurts business. He once said, "A man like Konosuke Matsushita wouldn't have been called the god of management there. He wouldn't have been such a success." Matsushita is the example par excellence in Japan of hard work crowned by fabulous wealth and honors. Apprenticed at the age of nine to a charcoal room-heater dealer, he founded the Matsushita Electric empire and became Japan's leading industrialist. He also typified the owner-manager company president.

In Japan, companies are either family owned and managed

or there is a psychological solidarity between the shareholders and management. In the United States, professional managers run the company for the stockholders, who often become adversarial if dividends slide. What are the consequences of these different arrangements?

According to Akio Morita, "The United States looks ten minutes ahead while Japan looks ten years ahead." U.S. executives with a short-term perspective frantically shift assets around to increase quarterly profits. Management expert Peter Drucker has criticized America's "symbol economy" of numbers without substance. Obsessed with mergers and acquisitions, many managers have neglected their companies' primary activities. Drucker has written that many U.S. corporations are doomed unless they return to a real economy where investment and profits are based on producing goods or services. That certainly makes sense to Japanese.

Managers who pursue immediate profits miss out on larger midterm (ten-year) gains. But U.S. institutional investors do not care where a company will be a decade from now. They are only interested, Morita says, in getting a quick, high return on their capital. If earnings fall off a bit, the big boys unload the stock before its value drops. Americans should listen to Morita.

Two U.S. studies make the same point: *Made in America: Regaining the Productive Edge*, published by the Massachusetts Institute of Technology in 1989, and the earlier *Global Competition: The New Reality*, by the President's Commission on Industrial Competitiveness, chaired by John A. Young, president and CEO of Hewlett-Packard Co. These reports have a wealth of information on how the United States can improve industrial productivity, but relatively few U.S. firms have heeded the advice from their own compatriots.

Among the outstanding exceptions are Caterpillar Inc., Cummins Engine Co., and Florida Power and Light, which have corrected their mistakes. Nearly all the rest frantically continue to play the money game.

The Rockefeller Group Inc.'s sale of Rockefeller Center to Mitsubishi Estate Co. for $846 million is an example. RGI executives decided they could make quicker profits by investing their money in stocks, bonds, and money-market accounts than from real estate holdings. RGI approached a total of seventeen Japanese firms, including Mitsubishi, Mitsui Real Estate Development Co., and Sumitomo Realty & Development Co. Finally, Mitsubishi agreed to purchase the complex.

Playing the financial market does not help an industry manufacture products or render services; in the long run, it only weakens a company. This phenomenon recently reared its ugly head in Japan, too, and the government is considering a capital gains tax and other measures to cool the speculative fever. The authorities are acting because a preoccupation with quick paper profits saps managerial energy.

In a great many of the U.S. corporations with a "ten-minute" mentality, ownership and management are completely divorced. Stockholder demands for high dividends not only encourage management to play the money game but also hamper efforts to enhance profitability through research and development (R&D), new products, boosting sales, and gradually acquiring a larger market share. Admittedly, Matsushita Electric is an unusual case of the "ten-year" approach. When an entrepreneur like Konosuke Matsushita not only owns the company but personally runs it and is responsible for operations, including the livelihood of thousands of employees, he must have a long-term vision. The employment contract of the average American CEO is for only a few years. If profits dip, he is quickly sent packing. The system forces the president to concentrate exclusively on short-term gains. This is the basic difference between the frenetic style of U.S. corporations and the relatively long-term approach of Japanese firms that stress steady market expansion.

I am not suggesting that Japanese companies are in all respects superior to U.S. firms. However, I do feel that the United States would be better off if the strident critics of Japan, who seem resentful of our economic growth, would shut up for a while and do their homework. They should analyze objectively what makes Japanese companies tick, study the solid suggestions to improve productivity made by American experts, and use this data to turn U.S. firms around.

The MIT Commission on Industrial Productivity listed six areas where U.S. industry is weak compared with Japan: (1) outdated strategies; (2) neglect of human resources (great class differences); (3) failures of cooperation (the United States leads the world in basic research for high technology but the results are not effectively utilized by industry and "poor communication and coordination" impede the flow of ideas and requests from factories to research centers); (4) technological weaknesses in development and production; (5) government and industry working at cross-purposes; and (6) short-term horizons.

A long-term perspective in dealing with stockholders and setting prices with subcontractors—the supplier-manufacturer nexus—is the underlying strength of Japanese industry. Many U.S. companies, driven by shareholder demands for profits, adopt management methods at odds with their raison d'être: to make goods or provide services. American businesses should heed Peter Drucker's maxim that management encompasses all technology.

I hope the United States is not too proud to roll up its sleeves and do whatever is necessary to revive its manufacturing industry and economy. Then, America's enormous potential in high-technology fields will bloom and contribute to the next era. U.S. attacks on Japan's trade practices and demands for reforms are not a black-and-white issue; some points are valid and others are not. One thing, however, is certain: American critics should take a cold shower and calm down.

Newsweek said of Sony's $3.4 billion purchase of Columbia Pictures that "this time the Japanese hadn't just snapped up another building; they had bought a piece of America's soul." But who put it up for sale? The attacks on Mitsubishi Estate Co. were equally unfair. Hajime Tsuboi, chairman of Mitsui Real Estate, told me at the time, "The Rockefeller Group offered the site to us, too. They initiated and pushed the deal. To me, as a Japanese, the negative American reaction is very regrettable." A few days later, Sumitomo Realty chairman Taro Ando gave me a similar account.

There is a widespread feeling in the United States that Japan is buying up America. The sentimental attachment to a Hollywood institution like Columbia Pictures and a New York landmark like Radio City Music Hall is understandable. But the American public, and Japanese who attacked these purchases as provocative, should realize that it takes two to make a deal: Americans put these properties on the market.

Some Americans will still object to rich Japanese companies picking up trophy real estate in Hawaii, Los Angeles, Dallas, and elsewhere. But look at the genesis of this situation. Aside from the general excellence of Japanese-style management, there was a more immediate factor. The U.S. currency-rate policy, broached in 1985 at a meeting of the finance ministers and central bankers of the major industrialized nations (the so-called Group of Five, or G-5), made Japan a financial superpower and Washington's creditor. Japan got those billions of dollars to buy real estate as a direct result of the Reagan administration's weak-dollar, strong-yen policy.

The strategy resembled the U.S. Occupation's grand design for postwar Japan in that initial success was followed by monumental failure. As a result of our U.S.-designed pacifist Constitution, which for practical political reasons cannot be revised, Japan made itself into the kind of country Washington wanted: an industrial nation that follows the U.S. lead in foreign policy and poses no military threat to anyone. But our manufacturing sector now outshines U.S. companies.

Similarly, Reagan's devaluation of the greenback made U.S. exports more competitive and reduced the current account deficit. At the same time, however, the United States became the world's largest debtor nation. Under present circumstances, no matter what steps the United States takes to revitalize its economy, by 1995, its net debt to Japan will be at least $1.3 trillion and our total net investment in the United States will be $700 billion.

Two trillion dollars is a lot of money, and conceivably the figure might go higher. Even if you subtract the profits of U.S. subsidiaries in other countries, the interest payments on that debt will be a huge burden. At 6 percent per annum, they will be equivalent to a 1 percent annual increase in the U.S. gross national product. It is a vicious circle of deficits, debt, and staggering interest payments.

The U.S. federal budget deficit is being slowly brought under control, but corporate debt is soaring. In 1987–89, the ratio of corporate indebtedness to the GNP rose dramatically, and that money is not being used in ways that will pay off later. The U.S. share of the world's GNP has fallen from 36 percent to 23 percent, while Japan's has risen from 6 percent to 16 percent, another consequence of the U.S.'s weak-dollar, strong-yen policy. These figures should be borne in mind as we plan for the future, allowing for the fact that numbers do not tell the whole story.

Strange as it may seem, U.S. demands on Japan boomerang; our concessions adversely affect the United States. That is precisely why, when circumstances warrant, we must resolutely say no to Washington. Firmness in Tokyo should speed America's economic recovery. The fall of dictators in Eastern Europe shows the fate of those who surround themselves with yes-men.

Mesmerized by junk bonds and leveraged buyouts, top U.S. management has contributed to the decline in American competitiveness. Profligate indebtedness has replaced frugality. Many executives seem uninterested in making profits the old-fashioned way: earning them with reliable products at affordable prices. Lee Iacocca, to cite one, was considered U.S. presidential timber, but by Japanese standards he is an unethical manager. In a cynical betrayal of American motorists, he took advantage of the appreciated yen that made imported Japanese cars more expensive, and jacked up the price of Chrysler cars. Iacocca also received huge bonuses after Chrysler employees had agreed to give-backs to save the company. Japanese managers are not immune to the lure of quick killings from stock and real estate speculation, but we can still head off such excesses.

American executives and politicians are foolishly offering unsolicited advice to Japan when their own industrial policies have strayed so far from sound business principles. Japan did not acquire its financial might through unfair methods. We earned our current-account surpluses. No other country should object to the purposes or methods, for example, of our Official Development Assistance (ODA). After all, it is our money. We should act to benefit the world community; however, the decisions on priorities and programs are our call, not Washington's. The suggestion, for example, that Japan and the United States provide billions of dollars to the Aquino government to compensate wealthy Philippine landowners whose plantations would be confiscated in a land reform was extremely naive. Good intentions taken this far dissolve into ludicrous giveaways. The Japanese public ought to know that many of the orders from Washington on how we should use our ODA are of this magnitude of incompetence.

Incidentally, Japan plans to provide approximately $6.5 billion in ODA from 1988 to 1992, an average of $1.3 billion annually. This is two and a half times the GNP of the Philippines and one-third that of Thailand. Nomura Securities has also established a $100 million Philippine Fund, to the delight of President Cory Aquino.

The United States may deplore Japan's status as the world's creditor, but it happened because Reagan administration policy backfired. Japanese have the flexibility to adjust quickly to any new situation. Americans push us around and think, "We've beat them this time." But we are a persistent people. We bear the unbearable, keep plugging away, and eventually accomplish our goals. When we dig in our heels, sometimes, Americans would be wise to back off.

We cannot cavalierly reject all U.S. trade demands, of course. But if both sides took tough positions, we on the FSX, for example, and the Bush administration on the Structural Impediments Initiative (SII) trade talks, the result would be a more positive relationship. Economic issues with large amounts of money at stake bring out the worst in Tokyo and Washington. It seems to the Japanese that U.S. emotionalism over Columbia Pictures and Rockefeller Center is a result of the Americans shooting themselves in the foot. In 1985, U.S. leaders were laughing up their sleeves at the dollar depreciation scheme they had foisted on Tokyo. It somehow misfired and instead made Japan affluent. Americans should follow the Chinese proverb, "When things go wrong, first look in the mirror."

CHAPTER 8

Saying Yes to America

[ALTHOUGH I strongly believe we should stand up to America], there are times, of course, when we should compromise. [There are also times when we should say yes when American demands obviously serve the mutual interest of both our countries.] During a dinner in Tokyo with Glenn Fukushima, a Harvard-educated Japan specialist who is with the Office of the U.S. Trade Representative, I asked what trade issues Washington was going to take up next. Fukushima said perhaps the distribution system, adding that without U.S. pressure, Japanese politicians could not change it. Galling though it is to think that we need a helping hand from the United States, Japan's complex wholesale and retail distribution channels are a knotty problem. An army of middlemen drive consumer prices sky high. Many organizations and special interests, not to mention politicians, make a living from this labyrinth.

We cannot brusquely reject all U.S. trade demands. Allowing U.S. rice into the Japanese market is a symbolic issue, pitting free-trade principles against protectionism. Urban areas like the district I represent do not object, but the countryside is dead set against any liberalization of import policies. "Not one grain of foreign rice" is the farmers' rallying cry.

Takashi Sato, minister of agriculture, forestry and fisheries in the Takeshita cabinet, argued Japan's case against liberalizing the import policies governing farm products. Despite my respect for Sato, his insistence that food self-sufficiency is essential for national security is no longer convincing. The global economy is interdependent today. President Jimmy Carter did not block grain sales to Moscow even when the Soviet Union had invaded Afghanistan. Midwest farmers probably lobbied vigorously against such an embargo. Japan is an even better customer; no U.S. administration could cut off food sales to us. Opponents of liberalizing rice import policies use a sentimental argument— rice cultivation is a cultural tradition. It is true that inefficient Japanese farmers might not be able to compete against U.S. agribusiness, with the result that the countryside would change. Nevertheless, we must give U.S. rice growers access to our market.

Public works projects also have to be opened to foreign construction firms. The handwriting is on the wall: More foreign companies are going to set up operations in Japan. It is an open secret that bid-rigging by general contractors in Japan raises the cost of public works projects about 40 percent higher than in Europe or the United States. Other countries are attacking the construction industry's exclusionist practices. Reforms must be carried out.

Saying No to Japanese

Americans used to champion equal opportunity; now their
trade officials have started calling for equal results, a change
they would probably attribute to Japan's "closed" market.
Excessive regulations and restrictions on U.S. products
should be removed, but managed trade is not the answer.
Economic activity not driven by market forces soon loses mo-
mentum. Today, companies must compete against rivals the
world over, not just against other domestic firms. Insisting
upon equality of results—reverse quotas or mandatory
purchasing—on the grounds that Japan's economic and political systems are different would soon undermine the vitality of
U.S. companies. Why should they become more efficient and
competitive if they have a captive market?

In a far-ranging discussion I had recently with Ronald
Morse, a Japan specialist then at the Library of Congress, he
acknowledged that trade friction between Japan and the
United States is actually a consequence of the U.S. political
and economic system. Morse said that Americans should wake
up to the fact that the $49 billion trade deficit with Tokyo is
essentially their own fault.

Much of what the United States buys from Japan is not
finished goods but parts for products assembled in the United
States and sold under U.S. brand names. Our industries are
offshore factories for U.S. manufacturers. Japan's economic
strength and U.S. competitive weakness are not a simple ab-
stract comparison; the two economies are so intertwined that
if the Japanese government bows to the Bush administration
on those trade demands that I think are reasonable, our industry will become even stronger. So far, every economic
concession wrung from Japan has had that result. According
to the report by the President's Commission on Industrial

Competitiveness, the more open the Japanese market has become, the more defeats U.S. manufacturers have suffered. High-pitched demands for complete trade liberalization may only make Japanese companies leaner and tougher.

This probable outcome, however, should not be used to justify a refusal to open our markets. We cannot be a closed society; interaction with the rest of the world should be our goal. Unreconstructed protectionists must be told unequivocally that foreign products can no longer be excluded from our shores. We have to say no to both the hypercritical elements in Washington and the old-fashioned types in Tokyo who think this country can still export without importing. For the sake of the great majority of Japanese, our politicians must rebuff the special interest groups.

Some Japanese attack the Structural Impediments Initiative talks, the bilateral trade negotiations held in 1989–90, as U.S. interference in our domestic affairs. I do not agree. Yelling "foreign pressure, foreign pressure" whenever the government negotiates is a timeworn ploy. There are countless protectionist strongholds that can only be breached with a push from outside. Our distribution system is one.

American businessmen and officials have raised this issue for several years, and rightly so. It is true that even Agatha Christie's Hercule Poirot would be baffled by how goods in Japan get from the factory or farm to the consumer. A thorough streamlining of distribution channels would make at least 300,000 people redundant. They would not be unemployed long, however. With the current labor shortage, all these people would quickly find new jobs. It is the consumer who deserves our sympathy. The personnel costs of the multi-tiered wholesale channels and small retail outlets make prices very high. Corporations may be getting rich, but Japan is very far from being an affluent society. It has been clear for some time that the disparity between our GNP and the average person's standard of living must be reduced through lower prices. Unfortunately, nothing has been done because many politicians have a financial stake in defending special interests.

Everyday things cost too much. In urban areas, a cup of coffee is ¥500 (about $3.50), an insane price. Japan's premier products—cameras, cosmetics, and consumer electronic goods—cost 20 percent more here than in New York or Los Angeles. With such absurd anomalies, no wonder people suspect that cartels set prices and manufacturers dump their products in the United States.

This eerie contradiction attests to how complicated Japan's distribution arrangements are. Consumers, especially the urban salaried strata, are the forgotten people, the victims of criminal neglect by the political process. Politicians must get involved and help shape a popular consensus against exorbitant prices. A 1989 report by the Economic Planning Agency (EPA) showed that typical consumer goods were an average of 40 percent higher in Tokyo than in New York. The items that were far more expensive in Japan were all subject to government regulation. The differential in a market basket of items meant that at equivalent salaries, a Tokyoite can purchase 40 percent less than a New Yorker. A white-collar employee in Otemachi earning a monthly wage at ¥400,000 ($2,857, at ¥140 = $1) can afford a life-style comparable to a Manhattan resident making ¥240,000 ($1,714) monthly. Lowering prices 40 percent would be like getting a ¥160,000 ($1,142) raise. Access to inexpensive goods and services is the key to a higher standard of living.

Bureaucrats and politicians justify their benign neglect of the consumer by saying that the high price structure is a "peculiarly Japanese phenomenon." We should not abandon the intangible, idiosyncratic qualities that sustain our economy—Japanese-style management and employees' intense commitment to a company—for American methods or values. However, preserving dysfunctional practices in the name of Japan's cultural identity is contemptible. Deregulation as a result of prodding by our trading partners has given shoppers a choice of less expensive and better products. And our culture remains intact.

The dispute over approving U.S.-made car phones symbolized anachronistic bureaucratic prerogatives. Ministry of Posts and Telecommunications officials insisted they controlled the radio waves and could regulate car phones, essentially denying market access to an American company. I have a Japanese-made phone in my car that is unreliable. It often goes dead in the middle of a conversation. If a large truck pulls up next to me at a traffic light or I go under the elevated highways that crisscross Tokyo, the phone does not work. Even the best Japanese phone can be easily monitored. Gangsters reportedly listened in when a certain politician was talking to his mistress and blackmailed him for a princely sum. Eavesdropping is so easy that no one would dare discuss a confidential matter on a car phone. U.S. models are supposed to be really good and I wanted to get one, but I was foiled by red tape. Warped bureaucratic logic has denied countless products and cost-savings to the Japanese consumer.

Pervasive bid rigging, known as *dango*, on public works projects is another officially condoned rip-off of the taxpayers. Prearranged bids run the cost 15 to 20 percent above that for comparable jobs in the private sector. Let the people see in whose pockets their money ends up. Despite foreign criticism of collusive bidding, the Ministry of Construction insists that the practice is essential to "maintain order in the industry." I would like to hear an explanation, no matter how tortured, of how this conspiracy serves the public interest. Far from trying to lower prices, officialdom helps to keep them sky high.

A bureaucrat even pooh-poohed the data on price differentials between Japan and other countries by saying, "Government ministries do not decide prices. Consumers do." A TV commentator retorted, "In other words, as long as somebody is willing to pay the price, it doesn't matter what the manufacturer or store charges!" Bureaucrats side with the producers and sellers and ignore the direct link between prices and the people's well-being. This inequity must stop.

If the ultimate purpose of national wealth is a higher standard of living and fulfillment for individuals, then the government must try to ease the burden of the high cost of basic necessities. The first step is deregulation, getting the bureaucrats out of the marketplace. Agreements on many of the U.S. demands in SII will benefit Japanese consumers.

In the future, political parties must stress the interests of consumers over those of producers, or risk rejection by the voters, no matter what other programs they advocate. Reorienting priorities would be a very effective way to resolve many of the trade issues with Washington.

In an exchange I had with American journalist James Fallows, he spoke of Japan's insatiable economic expansion. I think I can explain what makes Japanese run economically. Let us look at what happened when quotas on imported beef were expanded. Japanese trading firms in Australia bought up livestock ranches to corner the new market. Why couldn't those firms buy beef from Australian producers? Why do they almost compulsively exploit every opportunity to make more profit? The answer, I think, lies in the poor quality of life of individual Japanese employees. What to Westerners looks like corporate voracity actually is collective avarice to compensate for individual spiritual poverty. Workaholic behavior is a symptom, not a cause. Enhancing the individual's life would end this sublimation, this attempt to find personal satisfaction through the corporation's success and higher profits. It should also bring a new maturity to our society. As a people, Japanese have developed a very sophisticated spiritual culture—the tea ceremony, Noh, Zen, and the martial arts, to mention a few aspects. However, frustrated by the gulf between this metaphysical dimension and their mundane, uninspired daily lives, Japanese pour their energy into accomplishing corporate objectives.

Our national goal from the nineteenth century was to modernize and catch up with the West. It was only in the last decade when we surpassed the United States in certain fields that Japanese became aware of how totally we had committed ourselves to work and economic expansion. We are now at a historic turning point: We must shift from the enrichment of the corporation to the fulfillment of the individual. This will take innovative thinking about everything from politics to lifestyles.

To the United States, which is ahead of Japan in quality of life as measured by leisure, standard of living, and cultural infrastructure—museums, concert halls, theaters, philanthropic foundations—this means long-overdue reforms in Japanese business practices. But first there must be political change. Washington, ever mindful of the trade figures, will probably say, "We can't wait any longer." Nonetheless, Japan is just becoming aware of what a truly mature society is and the political agenda to achieve it.

Based on this newfound understanding, Japanese will have to reexamine the place of the company in their lives and society. We should quickly reform the tax system to encourage what Americans call corporate citizenship—the obligation of management to set aside a portion of profits to benefit society through charitable and cultural activities.

These individual- and consumer-oriented improvements in our standard of living are closely linked to the trade negotiation with the United States. We must reject the special pleading about "unique Japanese practices that have evolved over the centuries" and say no to old-fashioned bureaucrats and politicians who speak for entrenched interests. Saying yes to Washington on many issues is the way to improve ties with the United States.

CHAPTER 9

Japan and America: The Major Players in the New Era

THE HANDSHAKE between George Bush and Mikhail Gorbachev opening the Malta summit signaled the end of the cold war, the titanic clash between communism and democracy. Bush reacted ambivalently to the earlier East German decision to tear down the Berlin Wall. Although he praised the act, his face betrayed mixed emotions. A unified Germany will probably be a troublesome factor in U.S. plans.

Bush was discomfited by the rapid collapse of communism. The political experiment Lenin launched almost one hundred years ago was so contrary to human nature that it should have failed sooner. Yet a century is a mere instant in the saga of Homo sapiens, about long enough for a flawed idea to run its course.

Bush's perplexed look as the Berlin Wall came tumbling down evinced the confusion people feel in the transition from one era to another, whether they welcome or deplore the shift. The unfamiliar is disorienting. Nevertheless, societies, like individuals, change with the passage of time; the surging tides of history transform civilizations. Nations that fail to adjust lose control of their own destinies.

Buffeted by events, ties between countries ebb and alter. There is no permanent bilateral status quo. To ignore this evolution is at least imprudent, if not arrogant or ignorant. The Japan-U.S. relationship will also change in the future. Although the two countries have been very close since World War II, it has not always been marked by full mutual understanding. The current discord could become deep mistrust on both sides. That worst-case scenario can be avoided by regular in-depth contact and continued efforts to fathom each other's realities.

The United States has not sufficiently appreciated Japan or even taken us all that seriously, because since 1945, we have been under Uncle Sam's thumb. Today, Americans may feel that Japan is getting out of hand. My own view is that Japan should not immediately disassociate itself from the U.S. security system. For our sake and that of the whole Pacific region, the special Tokyo-Washington relationship must be preserved. A breakup could destroy the budding new developments in that region. Japan should play an expanded role in the post–cold war world order. Effective use of our economic power—technology, management skills, and financial resources—at our own initiative can be the key to stable progress.

The economic dimension of the next era is already unfolding. That communism, a political doctrine no longer meaningful or functional, has remained powerful until recently is an irony of history. Prolonged obsession with ideology was a cultural lag between technology and the human beings who created it. To Japanese, as a pragmatic people inclined toward craftsmanship rather than metaphysics, the end of ideology is good news.

History shows that technology creates civilization and determines the scale and level of its economic and industrial development. Eastern Europe and the Soviet Union want state-of-the-art technology and financial aid to make them productive. What country can provide them? Only Japan. But we cannot meet this challenge alone. It must be a joint undertaking with our partner, the United States.

Japan's World Role

In its opinions about Japan, Washington is divided into the so-called Cherry Blossom Club and the Japan-bashers, with the former in the departments of State and Defense and the latter headquartered on Capitol Hill. The U.S. military and foreign service are well aware that Japan's high technology and mass-production system are indispensable to America's global strategy and consider the torrent of congressional attacks unwise. Still, the Cherry Blossoms and the Japan-bashers agree on one thing: They do not want Japan to become more powerful than it is now.

Ronald Morse, a Japan specialist at the Library of Congress, and Alan Tonelson, former editor of *Foreign Policy*, coauthored an unusually freewheeling article in *The New York Times* entitled "Let Japan Be Japan" (October 4, 1987). They wrote: "Clearly, Japan should stand on its own two feet, strategically and politically as well as economically. By continuing to treat Japan as a subordinate, America only makes the inevitable breakup speedier and nastier." Morse and Tonelson concluded that "If Japan assumes a constructive role in regional and world affairs, both countries will benefit."

The message is clear: We must think and act for ourselves and stop being a dutiful underling who leaves all the hard decisions up to the boss.

At the risk of repeating myself, the first step in that direction is to get rid of our servile attitude toward the United States. We should no longer be at Washington's beck and call. The ending of *The King and I* suggests a great beginning for Japan. As his father is dying, the young son who will become king proclaims a new era for Siam: No longer will the subjects bow like toads. They will stand erect, "shoulders back and chin high," and look the king in the eye as a proud people were meant to do.

Once Japanese stands up to Uncle Sam, what will we do with our independence? What ideals do we bring to the global arena?

When Emperor Hirohito died in January 1989 and his son Akihito acceded to the throne, a new era—*Heisei*, or "achievement of peace"—was proclaimed that symbolizes Japan's role in the future course of civilization. The two characters that make up the word *Heisei* appear in such classical passages as "Tranquility achieved inside makes the outside peaceful." Japan's stability and progress will be increasingly intertwined with those of the outside world. This will be the first time Japanese play a leading role on the world stage, a task to which I think we are equal and must accept. The cooperation of many other nations, foremost among them the United States, is essential.

Some scholars say that in peacetime relations between nations do not change overnight. Nevertheless, in a period of great historical upheaval like the present, there are seminal events that alter our perceptions of the world. To the careful observer, history provides valid principles for a nation's course of action and approach. The echoes of the past reverberate for a while, but it is only the past, after all. Our task is to define the elusive future, to hear those faint portentous sounds of tomorrow. We look back at history to see ahead.

As the tempestuous twentieth century draws to a close, I would like to add a postscript to modernism. Caucasians deserve much credit in the creation of modern civilization, but they were not the only agents of change. Historian Arnold J. Toynbee patronizingly called Japan's rapid modernization a miracle. Bedazzled by the swift transformation from a feudal, agricultural society into an industrial and military power, Toynbee concluded that we had simply imitated the West. Regrettably, some Japanese agree with the British scholar's interpretation and are delighted at this "high praise." This sad lot does not understand history. What to superficial observers seems like the instantaneous aping of Western ways was actually the fruition of innumerable cultural advances over the course of many centuries.

The modernization that started in Japan in the late nineteenth century was built upon the highly sophisticated culture of the Tokugawa period (1603–1867), which in turn evolved from the Azuchi-Momoyama culture of the late sixteenth century that was so admired by Spanish and Portuguese priests and merchants. Yoshimasa Ashikaga's (1436–90) aesthetic splendor graced the fifteenth century and so on back a millennium. How preposterous to assert that somehow modern Japan sprang full-blown from Western seeds! China dates from antiquity but lacks cultural continuity and consistency because of dynastic upheaval and foreign rule. In contrast, Japan's superior cultural ethos enabled us to modernize successfully. Toynbee, whether intentionally, unconsciously, or from ignorance, said nothing about this historical heritage.

At any rate, Japanese must understand that today the nation is riding the crest of a great historic wave and, with the United States, will shape the next age. I disagree with the oft-stated view that the twenty-first century will be a penta-polar world—the United States, Japan, Europe, the Soviet Union, and China. The United States will probably pull itself together and continue to be a leader. Eastern Europe and the Soviet Union, however, will ultimately be part of the global network of Japanese technology.

The United States wants to provide massive aid to Eastern Europe, such as the Marshall Plan that stimulated Western Europe's recovery after World War II. Many Americans trace their ethnic heritage to the Old World, and to keep the upper hand with Moscow, Washington should try to establish hegemony over the former Iron Curtain countries.

Mired in debt, however, the United States lacks the financial wherewithal to be the principal aid donor and will be unable to revive its economy and mount such an initiative until early in the twenty-first century. First there must be a massive federal program to improve the school system and retrain the labor force. The investment in human resource development will not pay off for at least fifteen years.

The Japanese have shown great technological competence, especially in commercializing and mass production of quality goods. The United States is ahead in many aspects of basic research, but brilliant breakthroughs in the laboratory are useless until engineers and lathe operators turn them into products. By bridging the gap between the ivory tower and the assembly line, Japanese know-how contributes to the world economy.

Here is the probable scenario for Eastern Europe: Our funds and technology will resuscitate the region. Then the former satellites will gradually transfer know-how to the Soviet Union, bringing it within our technological sphere of influence. From Tokyo to Moscow via Warsaw and Prague will be a short journey.

Sino-Soviet relations will probably remain less than fraternal. Moscow cannot demobilize its huge armed forces immediately. There are insufficient job openings in the civilian sector, and the whole Red Army cannot be sent back to the countryside to work on farms. The Kremlin will need a potential threat somewhere and China best fits the bill. Soviet forces may be deployed in greater strength along the Sino-Soviet border, making it a flash point again. Delicate Moscow-Beijing ties will complicate Japan's relations with China. If we have to choose between the two giants, we will probably lean toward the Soviet Union, which will have cast off rigid Marxist-Leninist ideology. For many years, some Japanese business leaders have expressed interest in the Soviet Union's natural resources and Siberia's market potential. This is not to make light of a billion Chinese, but given these realities, I anticipate Japan tilting toward the Soviet Union.

In the coming decades, Europe will be dominated by a reunited Germany. The Soviet Union and China will be less dynamic than at present, whereas the Pacific region and Southeast Asia will be more. The Japan-U.S. team must be a constructive influence in this new configuration.

The Kowtow Ministry

Both Japan and the United States are to blame for current bilateral tensions. To emphasize a point I touched upon earlier, the main villain in Tokyo is the Foreign Ministry. Japan cannot play its proper role in the world with diplomats who only know how to say to Washington, Beijing, and other world capitals, "Yes, fine, whatever you say." As minister of transport, I was involved in several incidents where the Foreign Ministry was incredibly submissive to other governments.

The first involved the Iran-Iraq conflict. Japan had developed a special relationship with Tehran, thanks to the efforts of former foreign minister and senior LDP leader Shintaro Abe. During the "tanker war" phase of the conflict, however, the United States vented on Japan its frustration at the course of events. The Reagan administration, saying it would provide additional protection to Japanese tankers, demanded that we support its policy toward Iran.

This was blatant interference in our affairs. Iran never attacked vessels flying the Japanese flag. A plan was worked out whereby Japanese ships formed into convoys at the mouth of the Persian Gulf. A liaison office in Abu Dhabi notified Iran each time Japanese tankers were about to enter the Strait of Hormuz, and they were given safe passage. The only Japanese sailors killed or wounded during the conflict were on ships of foreign registry.

Washington objected to this special arrangement and told us to stop. It was an unreasonable demand: Japanese lives, tankers, and oil supplies would have been put at risk. Instead of dismissing a proposal so harmful to Japan's national interests, timid Foreign Ministry officials asked my ministry's view of the matter. We immediately refused to alter the convoy scheme, and I strongly objected to the Foreign Ministry even bringing the matter to me for consultation.

My second run-in with the foreign service was over the U.S.S. *Towers*, the U.S. destroyer that held firing practice at the entrance of Tokyo Bay, sighting on a Maritime Safety Agency (MSA) vessel. I described earlier the Foreign Ministry's attempt to cover up the incident. Afterward, Richard L.

Armitage, deputy secretary of defense for international security affairs, apologized, and Washington also sent a high-ranking military officer to make amends. After expressing U.S. regrets to the prime minister and foreign minister, the emissary reportedly wanted to pay a call on me as well, since the MSA is under the Transport Ministry. Foreign Ministry officials, however, told him it was unnecessary, their way of getting even with me.

My third experience with the mealymouthed Foreign Ministry concerned China. In February 1987, a group of high school students from Kochi Prefecture on a school trip were involved in a train accident near Shanghai and more than thirty teenagers were killed. This is the inside story of the indemnity negotiations that followed.

Japanese parents asked for a solatium of about $210,000 per person and China offered $2,100. The family of one Chinese killed in the wreck received only $483. When the talks were stalemated, Akira Okamura, a lawyer and friend of mine, was named to head the parents' group seeking compensation. Premier Takeshita was scheduled to visit Beijing at this time, and at Okamura's behest, I asked him to raise the issue, which he did. I learned afterward that Premier Li Peng said, "I am concerned about the negotiations. Japan is so much richer than China that the requested amount is far out of line with what we can afford." In effect, Li appealed to Takeshita to have the parents reduce their claim.

At a press briefing after the two premiers met, reporters asked if Takeshita had discussed the compensation and, if so, Li's response. A Foreign Ministry spokesman for some reason replied, "The Chinese premier said he would do his best, in the interest of Sino-Japanese friendship." It was a bald-faced lie, exactly the opposite of what Li really said. Presumably, the spokesman hoped to curry favor with the Chinese by putting a good spin on the news. The Japanese press reported this disinformation, and when Okamura read it, he flew over to Beijing to open talks. Brandishing the report of Li's comment, he pressed for a suitable settlement. The Chinese, however, informed him that the account was erroneous and rejected his argument. Confused, Okamura met with a Foreign Ministry official and asked what Li had actually told Takeshita.

"We are under no obligation to report the details of such a meeting to private citizens like you," the official said imperiously, refusing to discuss the matter. The only explanation I can offer for this incomprehensible attitude is that our diplomats are always dealing with foreign countries and out of touch with their own. They are more worried about the reaction of other governments than about what Japan should do. A younger element in the Foreign Ministry is critical of this tendency, but their impact on policy is not yet apparent.

Institutional subservience dating from Japan's occupation after World War II has undercut our negotiating positions and ruined our foreign policy. A country must clearly articulate what it wants. The Foreign Ministry is such a weak spokesman for Japan that the Tokyo-handlers in Washington, Beijing, and elsewhere take advantage of this deferential unassertiveness.

Communication is terrible at the Foreign Ministry; the right hand does not know what the left is doing. There is little evidence of vertical or lateral coordination. The minister, a political appointee, is often ignored by the bureaucracy and excluded from the policy-making process. Each of these officials may take pride in representing Japan, but the age of swallow-tail coats and white gloves is long over. Today, style is less important than substance, and diplomats must be articulate and determined. An endemic inability even to communicate Japan's positions has been detrimental to our interests. Ultimately, the responsibility lies with the politicians who have allowed the civil servants too much latitude.

In summary, unless Japan can convey its views forcefully, other nations will assume that with enough pressure, Tokyo always caves in. This perception endangers our foreign relations. If we continue this kowtow diplomacy, one day it may be too late to say no. Nobody will take us seriously. After years of operating successfully on this premise, other nations will think it a bit late in the day for Japan to object.

A Partnership for the World

Japan's foreign policy is obviously inadequate for a world in flux. I reiterate this point as a warning to the Japanese people, who are complacent after more than four decades of peace and prosperity and now might have to make very hard choices on short notice. Seeing how people are preoccupied with their vested interests, regional or industrial, and fight tooth and nail to protect the status quo, I am not sure the nation is ready for a new role in the post-détente era.

A comment about the cold war by Raymond Aron, the French educator and writer, comes to mind—that peace is unattainable but war is impossible. With the Malta thaw, that observation can be updated to peace has been obtained but war is possible. An East-West conflict would have escalated to an all-out nuclear exchange, so a major showdown was avoided. Regional clashes, however, remain a great danger. In a sense, the world is more complicated now. As political scientist Yonosuke Nagai has said, "Diplomacy will be extremely important to Japan from now on." Also, with the shift from military confrontation to economic competition, Japan needs a national strategy for global trade relations.

The conflicts among nations will be increasingly economic in nature. With the cold war over, friction on trade and investment will inevitably intensify. Over the next few years, Japan-bashing in the United States will become even more virulent. Although I see the bilateral relationship as the dominant force in the next century, before we reach that level of cooperation, U.S. policy toward Japan will approximate the stance against the Soviet Union at the height of the cold war.

First, Americans will argue that Japan is different and therefore a threat. Next, a "collective security system" will be created to block Japan's economic expansion. Then protectionist measures and sanctions against Japanese products will follow one after the other. An alliance is already being formed against Japan. Finally, there will be a witch hunt directed at everything Japanese. We must be prepared for stormy days ahead.

If we try to bend with the wind, making concessions and patchwork compromises as usual, the tempest will abate for a while, only to recur with even greater force. We must not flinch in the face of pressure. The only way to withstand foreign demands is to hold our ground courageously. No more temporizing. When justified, we must keep saying no and be undaunted by the reaction, however furious. A prolonged standoff forces both sides to find areas of agreement. That is the best way to resolve disputes, not unilateral concessions by Japan, which leave the other party unaware of how we really feel. Our lack of assertiveness in the past has led to disparaging epithets like "the faceless people."

Our "yes, yes" style of diplomacy limits freedom of action and confuses the public. Koichiro Asakai, former ambassador to the United States, writing in the Hitotsubashi University alumni journal, has decried our concession-prone foreign policy and continued deference to the United States. For example, suppose a Soviet foreign minister said, "We will return the four northern islands. You abrogate the Japan-U.S. security treaty. The Soviet Union is no threat to Japan." A certain segment of the public would welcome the Soviet proposal. How would politicians respond to Moscow and approach Washington? A misstep might cause a political upheaval in Japan, according to Asakai, and he wondered whether the government had the gumption to make the first move.

A deal with the Soviet Union over semiconductors cannot be completely ruled out. As I have noted, microchips determine the accuracy of weapons systems and are the key to military power. U.S. strategists count on Japan's ability to mass produce quality chips. Yet some Japanese businessmen believe that if Moscow returns the Northern Territories, we should terminate the security treaty and become neutral. They hope Japan would then receive exclusive rights to develop Siberia.

Quite conceivably the Soviet Union would prefer tie-ups with Japan in some areas over the United States. We have maglev technology for a high-speed rail network in Siberia, which the United States does not, and are ahead in some other major high-tech fields, too. We should indicate to the Americans that Tokyo and Moscow have this option. However, even saying this to Washington is, at present, out of the question for the Japanese establishment.

But politicians and bureaucrats must realize that the time is past when Japan can be preoccupied with its own affairs. For the past forty-five years we have not had a major say in world developments. Geopolitical factors always dictated a reactive stance. Playing the leading man is out of character. Nevertheless, stage fright will keep us in the wings forever. If we know our lines and say them confidently, I am sure our performance will get rave reviews. After all, we are not an unknown understudy. Our long history and rich culture have prepared us for the limelight.

Japan-bashing is a reaction both to our moving to center stage and the impending Pacific Century. Only the uninformed or insolent would say we are unqualified for leadership. That the United States, our indispensable partner, is furiously attacking us is extremely regrettable.

It is true that postwar Japan has not taken major political initiatives. To say, however, that the country is incapable of lofty goals or thinks only of self-interest shows utter contempt for Japan. A well-funded creative aid program that combined high technology with management expertise could be the core of a Japanese vision.

Washington's present control over our Official Development Assistance funds shows a lack of respect for Japan's autonomy. I wonder if the American public is aware and approves of this maddening situation. A country desirous of obtaining aid from Japan first sounds out the United States; we disburse the funds as Washington directs, including support for some worthless projects. According to Ronald Morse, this setup evolved because Japanese leaders did not tell aid-seekers that Tokyo makes the decisions. But actually, our prime ministers could not say that without offending the United States. Nor is this interference in our internal affairs an isolated case. Washington has prevented every bid by Japan to purchase reconnaissance satellites.

Henry Kissinger, now a foreign affairs entrepreneur, has recently been demagogically raising the specter of a Japanese military threat. To justify the continued presence of U.S. forces in Asia despite local objections, he and others reportedly have said that Japan will fill the vacuum left by a U.S withdrawal from the region. To Japanese, this is world-class nonsense, but in view of the past, it may have a certain credibility in Southeast Asia. Has the United States degenerated to the point where it can only retain influence in the region by portraying Japan as a bogeyman?

The United States has frustrated virtually every independent foreign policy overture Japan has attempted. The Occupation is long over; it is time for parity. Washington must reappraise its avuncular superiority toward Japan and its own position in the world, and adopt a new outlook.

Industrial Robots and the Tea Ceremony

For some time I have proposed that Japan and the United States form a Super Group of Two analogous to the Group of Seven major industrialized nations. The two leading economic powers must coordinate and cooperate in many areas, from trade to the environment. Unquestionably, the United States is the cutting-edge country in high technology. Yet as Peter Drucker says, technology must be combined with management. Granted a U.S. lead in basic research, Japan skillfully links technology and management to make products for worldwide marketing. Japanese would bring very sophisticated assets to the G-2 team, resources the United States now lacks. Congressional acquaintances admit that the U.S. manufacturing sector is losing this dynamic dimension. We agree that Japan's strengths would complement those of the United States, and vice versa. My conversations in Washington show that even though Japanese and Americans start out at loggerheads, we can find areas of agreement. Thrashing matters out is the way to establish common ground.

Japan has plenty of other know-how to offer the United States, most notably corporate culture. Japanese companies are distinctive for their warm interpersonal relations. There is an emotional attachment to company, workplace, colleagues, and even the machinery. To cite an extreme case, workers affix photos of popular singers like Momoe Yamaguchi and Junko Sakurada to industrial robots and nickname the machines "Momoe" or "Junko." Silly as this may seem, it enhances productivity. Thinking of a cold piece of metal in human terms generates a kind of empathy, a personal connection. Employees regard the robots as coworkers and quickly spot and repair trouble. Less time is lost on the assembly line.

Many Japanese mistakenly think this emotional ambiance cannot be transferred abroad. Actually, it is relatively easy to do, especially compared with high culture like Noh, the tea ceremony, and flower arranging, rarefied tastes not easily acquired. Sharing our know-how in the industrial sphere is more efficient and useful. Understanding the emotional context of a Japanese-style factory provides some background for the refined aesthetics of the Way of Tea and ikebana. An appreciation of Japanese culture will lead to respect for Japan as a country. Despite my (undeserved) reputation as a troublemaker, I am always looking for constructive ways to present Japan to other countries.

Supinely saying "yes, yes" to every demand without presenting our case gets us nowhere. Too many Japanese deeply resent U.S. pressure but have confined their comments to grumbling in private. My outspokenness is considered a liability in Tokyo. Argument for argument's sake is not welcomed; people become offended and break off relationships. Every time I visit Washington or New York, where straight talk is respected, I realize anew the importance of directness.

I try to be absolutely explicit in my discussions in the United States. Many Americans have said, "You're a strange Japanese," or "I've never met a Japanese like you." Of course, they do not agree with everything I say, but at least we know what is on each other's minds. At this turning point in Japanese-American relations, indeed for the whole world, dialogue must start here.

CHAPTER 10

Looking Ahead in Europe and Asia

CONTRARY TO my hopes for a real partnership between Tokyo and Washington in 1989, the Bush administration forced Japan to participate in the SII talks, further evidence of the unequal relationship. The issues—alleged barriers to trade and investment—should have been taken up in the General Agreement on Tariffs and Trade (GATT), a multilateral forum, but Washington, insisting that its trade deficit with Japan be resolved, demanded bilateral talks.

The SII exercise has only delayed correction of the trade imbalance. In March 1990, while the talks were still under way, Michael Farren, undersecretary of commerce for international trade, reportedly told a Senate subcommittee that if Japan's market were fully opened, in a few years U.S. trade figures for Japan would be in the black, as was the case with the European Community. Farren was either telling the senators this nonsense because he simply does not understand the nature of Japan-U.S. economic relations, or it was what they wanted to hear. A third possibility, I suppose, is that he was trying to encourage them to keep the pressure on Tokyo. Whatever his motives, Farren's testimony bordered on fantasy.

Robert McNamara, former president of the World Bank, said recently that as long as American industry cannot compete internationally, liberalization of Japan's market will have no effect on the U.S. trade deficit with Tokyo. This was an objective, accurate, and responsible statement.

During the SII talks, the Japanese side recommended several steps to make the U.S. economy more competitive. U.S. officials flatly said no to some (such as an increase in the gasoline tax to reduce the federal deficit) and on others said that "the administration is taking action" but with an escape clause about the need for congressional approval.

Japan accepted almost all the unreasonable U.S. demands, even the outrageous one on public works spending. Although the administration of Toshiki Kaifu rejected the initial call for Japan to commit 10 percent of its GNP to public investment, it did promise to spend the staggering sum of ¥430 trillion ($2.9 trillion at ¥150 = $1) over the next ten years. The Finance Ministry opposed this pledge, saying that any sane economist would dismiss the idea with contempt, but it finally had to yield to the politicians and the Foreign Ministry.

Skillful use of public works spending to adjust the business cycle has been a factor in Japan's economic success. To ward off recession, the government has even drawn up emergency budgets and started public works projects ahead of schedule. Now, however, the economy is in a record-breaking expansionary phase. Massive public spending on top of a vigorous private sector causes shortages in materials, which in turn drive up prices, leading to wage increases, a decline in productivity, and inflation. What kind of bilateral relationship is it when the Japanese government announces it will commit economic suicide and the United States lauds this as "cooperation"? Japanese taxpayers will not buy this deal.

Washington's strategy is to use political pressure—the threat of sanctions—to disrupt and weaken Japan's economy and thereby improve America's position. But this beggar-thy-neighbor approach will not save America.

During a visit to the United States in May 1990, I spoke at Harvard University, the Brookings Institution, and to several groups concerned with foreign affairs. I received a sympathetic hearing and the audience reactions were enlightening. One point I reiterated everywhere was that although Japan and the United States are capitalist countries, their business practices and the role of government in the market are significantly different. The dissimilarities stem from history and culture. We must acknowledge that valid differences exist and compromise to transcend them or formulate new rules that both sides can live with.

Economics is a game of clear-cut results. When one team indisputably wins, the losers should admit their failure and try harder. If a high jumper developed a new back roll and shattered all existing records, competitors would practice day and night until they had mastered the technique. A willingness to learn from others and make adjustments is the mark of a champion. Several of the proposals made in the following chapter may require changes in the way things are done in the United States. The decision, of course, is up to the American people. In any case, these innovations will not undermine the American way of life.

Japan's experience is relevant here. In the mid-nineteenth

century, Commo. Matthew C. Perry helped awaken Japan to modern civilization, and we worked hard to absorb Western ideas, institutions, and technology. For a while, Japanese were ridiculed for imitating the West. However, we did not jettison our traditional culture and national identity. The same would be true of the United States if it adopted some suggestions from Japan to make its economy more competitive.

When Europe was at the height of its glory, Oswald Spengler wrote *The Decline of the West* and prophesied the end of the modern age. A great ideological experiment in the Soviet Union and Eastern Europe has utterly failed; the genesis of a new civilization is imminent. What we are witnessing today is not "the end of history" and the triumph of Western democracy, as an American writer has enthused. The odyssey of Alexander Solzhenitsyn, expelled from the Soviet Union but disenchanted with America, too, suggests that humankind's quest will continue.

Americans should realize the modern era is over. Their cherished beliefs in materialism, science, and progress have borne bitter fruit. The defeat in Vietnam, despite raining napalm and Agent Orange on the countryside for ten years, showed the futility of military power. America harnessed science and technology and spent a fortune to get to the moon, only to find a barren rock pile. All that money and effort and what does the nation have to show for it? And now, in economics, a very down-to-earth activity, Japan is outpacing the United States.

The sharp contrast between Japanese and American industry and business is not just in efficiency—production, distribution, and services—but is related to Eastern ways and values. Japan is both part of the capitalist world and Asian. It is a little late in the game for Americans to say Japan must change because it operates on a different set of principles, as the so-called revisionist critics do. We are in and of the Orient. Calling us an unfair trading nation because we do not do things the American way is a low blow.

Recent events mark the end of European modernity, including communism and socialism. Scientists have confirmed that even the universe is finite; our own planet Earth is on the verge of an environmental disaster. As Spengler predicted, the solution is to attain a higher level of civilization blended from diverse cultures. Our one hope is a dialectical leap forward into a new synthesis. The United States is a Western model of modern civilization, Japan an Eastern version. They are different but not incompatible; confrontation is not inevitable. Bearers of great traditions, both countries are now challenged to reach a higher level of human accomplishment.

In the new age, economics will be preeminent. Military might was all-important in the past, but, ironically, atomic weapons, with their mutually assured destruction, have changed that. Henceforth, economic power—industry, technology, and finance—will be decisive. If I am right, the Soviet Union and China, losers in economic competition, will not carry the same weight in world politics that they have in the past. I was astounded, for example, at the naïveté of Chinese economic officials. In conversations with several, I found that they did not understand the concept of interest or the relative importance of labor costs in productivity. They thought depreciation was simply the wear and tear on an item over time. Having no experience with a market economy, their Rip van Winkle state was understandable. Nevertheless, they are under a formidable handicap in the 1990s. I have heard that a Chinese scholar who plagiarized Adam Smith and John Stuart Mill was lauded as an economic genius and appointed to an important position!

I believe the twenty-first century will be a tripolar world—the United States, Japan, and Europe. Americans may try to reaffirm their historical ties to the lands of their forefathers, but the post-1992 European Community is likely to be noncommittal. Moreover, with a unified Germany in its midst, I strongly doubt that the European Community will be one big harmonious family. Age-old rivalries remain. A dominant Germany might spark British and French animosity. An even greater destabilizing factor would be a Moscow-Berlin axis. Imagine what would happen if the Soviet Union, with its great natural resources, managed through German help to shift to an efficient market economy.

The United States, perhaps from a sense of affinity with or compassion for a vanquished adversary, now welcomes the Soviet Union's modernization. The question mark is Kremlin enthusiasm for cozying up to the Americans. It is simplistic to think that an enduring Soviet-American relationship is being built on McDonald's hamburgers and Pepsi-Cola. Regardless of the intense longing Muscovites have for things Western—from freedom to jeans and rock 'n' roll—the Soviet leadership's primary concern lies with a powerful Germany. Given the traditional Russian awe of Deutschland, Berlin, not Washington, is the natural place to look for an alliance.

Mikhail Gorbachev said little about Germany during his June 1990 meeting with George Bush. His hidden agenda surely is to solicit from the United States tangible and intangible support in order to forge a tie-up with the Germans under the most advantageous terms. For the Russians know full well that the United States will not be part of the new Europe. Americans would do well to remember that.

It should be crystal clear to the United States that it is part of the Pacific community, a group of nations with far greater stability and potential than the rest of the Third World. Realizing, as former U.S. ambassador to Tokyo Mike Mansfield did, that their future lies along the Pacific Rim would profoundly alter American perceptions. The nation built by peoples from so many racial and ethnic backgrounds would achieve its destiny in the rich diversity of Asia. The United States would then be the central pillar in a tripolar world.

Japan can play a constructive role in Europe. Unlike the Bush administration, which wants Japanese to be spendthrifts, the International Monetary Fund applauds our propensity to save: Japanese funds are badly needed for aid to Eastern Europe and the Third World. We can offer a special kind of aid program that combines funds, management know-how, and technology.

Our relations with Europe are presently marred, however, by trade friction. Many countries have taken unilateral actions against Japanese products that are even harsher than those of the United States. European officials have interpreted laws and regulations in a highly arbitrary way, and governments have sabotaged liberalization agreements to protect their domestic industries. I hope these obstacles will be removed when Europe forms a single market.

Japan should concentrate aid to Eastern Europe on a few countries that meet certain criteria: an advanced society, experience with a market economy, and a relatively small-scale national economy. Czechoslovakia and Hungary are ideal candidates. An intensive effort should show impressive results within five years.

Neither Britain nor France should object to a Japanese presence. The lack of close ties with Prague and Budapest in the past may actually facilitate the programs. Not having colonized or invaded either country should be advantageous. Such initiatives are very important to demonstrate that Japan is a world leader and what it can accomplish. Success in East-

ern Europe would help overcome Southeast Asia's ambiva-
lence about Japanese aid.

With the end of modernism, Japanese and Americans are
like the explorers in the Age of Discovery: uncertain but in-
trepid, scanning the horizon for signs of the new age. We
must travel lightly on this journey, discarding useless posses-
sions like national stereotypes and prejudice. And for a safe
passage, we need the beacon of a closer equal partnership.

CHAPTER 11

An Agenda for
America

THE INTERIM report on the SII talks issued in April 1990 shows
that for the first time Japan made proposals to the United
States, although they were few in number and limited in scope
compared with the American list. The U.S. response, however, was vague and inconclusive. For the SII to be really productive, Japan should have pointed out the many drastic steps
the United States must take to become more competitive—
measures that are obvious to Japanese—and it should have requested action.

In the common interest of the two nations, I urge that the
Bush administration and the Congress act swiftly upon such
studies as *Global Competition: The New Reality* by the President's Commission on Industrial Competitiveness, the MIT
Commission on Industrial Productivity's *Made in America*,
and the Office of Technology Assessment's *Making Things
Better.* Implementing these recommendations would help
correct the bilateral trade imbalance.

In the SII talks, the U.S. side presented Japan with more than two hundred items for discussion, including some far-fetched suggestions that utterly ignored distinctive features of Japanese society, especially certain cultural aspects. Perhaps these were part of the trial-and-error process of serious negotiations. In any case, Japan should have made bolder and more specific proposals.

I and fifteen like-minded politicians who want U.S. industry to regain its competitive edge prepared an agenda of several specific proposals that should have been presented as friendly suggestions at the SII talks. I offer these suggestions here as a basis for discussion.

1. Savings and Investment

Japan has scrupulously honored the 1985 Plaza agreement. The government withstood domestic protectionist pressures and steadily opened Japan's market to foreign manufactured goods and services even more and revitalized the civilian sector through a sweeping relaxation of regulations that impeded economic activity. Japan has also carefully monitored the yen's exchange rate against the U.S. dollar and followed a flexible fiscal policy. The U.S. government, however, did not vigorously implement its side of the agreement and failed to fulfill its promises. The primary cause of America's financial malaise is excessive spending and consumption. Fiscal discipline must be restored now. The executive branch and Congress should cooperate closely to carry out the following proposals:

- Make vigorous efforts to cut the federal deficit through reduced expenditures and government savings.
- Establish a federal indirect tax.

- Strengthen the Gramm-Rudman-Hollings Budget Reduction Act.
- Create a Social Security Integrity and Debt Reduction Fund.
- Study the enactment of new taxes to increase revenue.
- Raise user fees for private and commercial aircraft and make the 3 percent communications tax permanent.
- Create family savings accounts.
- Improve Individual Retirement Accounts.
- Exempt the interest on small savings accounts from taxation.
- Lower the capital gains tax.
- Participate in savings/investment plans through payroll deductions.
- Reduce availability of automatic teller machine service to twelve hours daily.
- Establish a postal savings system.
- Restrain speculative investment by corporations and channel capital into productive sectors.
- Adopt measures to prevent speculative investment. For example, consider taxes and other disincentives to discourage hostile takeovers.
- Prohibit the resale for one year of a company acquired by merger.
- Stop excessive corporate takeovers. Revise the tax code to disallow counting interest payments on loans to finance takeovers as a loss and prohibit carry-forwards of more than two years.
- Curb leveraged buyouts.
- Regulate credit card use by raising handling charges and levying a tax.
- Punish severely such credit card abuses as improper use or payment delinquency.

- Shorten credit card payment-due periods.
- Tighten credit card eligibility criteria.
- Raise the minimum age.
- Shift wage and salary payments from weekly to monthly and introduce a bonus system.
- Prohibit the use of home-equity loans and home-purchase loans for other purposes.
- Study the imposition of a commodity tax focused on luxury goods.

2. Corporate Investment and Productivity

As the MIT Commission on Industrial Productivity has shown, one cause of America's economic woes is that government and industry are often at cross-purposes. Political leadership at the federal and state levels must work together so governmental actions will contribute to economic growth. No institutional link ensures cooperation between the White House and state houses. A clear division of responsibilities and close coordination are essential to formulate and implement consistent policies. The following specific proposals should also be considered:

- Revise antitrust laws to boost U.S. competitiveness.
- Standardize product liability laws nationwide and limit compensation amounts.
- Review government regulations concerning foreign direct investment (including nondiscriminatory treatment of Japanese firms) to ensure an open and equal investment policy.
- Reconfirm the nondiscriminatory treatment stipulated in tax treaties.

- Improve the after-service provided by automobile dealers.
- Expand overseas sales networks and service. American automobiles are plagued by mechanical failures within a few months. West German and other foreign-made cars have few breakdowns and are now selling in Japan at a rate six to seven times that of Detroit models.
- Prepare legislation to correct the priority accorded shareholders, including such measures as a maximum limit on dividends.
- Encourage management to have a long-run perspective. Consider tax incentives for long-term investment (e.g., accelerated depreciation).
- Discard the short-term, quick-profits mentality and follow a far-sighted strategy in plant and equipment investment. Revise laws governing corporations accordingly.
- Adopt a new management philosophy that stresses labor-management cooperation, anticipation of consumer needs, quality control, and technology and production processes.
- Conduct a national review of management outlook and methods under government auspices.
- Create a national council for labor-management cooperation with representatives from the public and private sectors.
- Study new tax incentives to encourage corporate investment in plant and equipment.
- Offer tax incentives to stimulate exploration of oil and gas deposits.
- Establish a federal agency to improve quality in manufacturing and assembly and set national standards. Move expeditiously toward unified, international standards acceptable to Japan and other nations.

- Consider measures, including legislation, to alter the disdain in management circles for hands-on manufacturing experience and bias in favor of financial or legal expertise.
- Reduce quarterly dividend payments to shareholders to twice yearly.
- Base U.S. requests for market access in Japan on competitive ability in a given sector. For example, U.S. construction firms should learn from their past failures, link up with local subcontractors, and have the requisite technology.
- Fully utilize robotics technology.
- Acknowledge that U.S. agricultural subsidies are more extensive than those in Japan—twice as high on a per capita basis and about five times as high per farm household—and that the United States restricts the import of farm products. If the U.S. government wants other nations to abolish agricultural subsidies, it should first eliminate its own.
- Abandon the insistence on bilateral trade balances.

3. Corporate Behavior

Managers must have a long-term perspective. Peter Drucker has written that management encompasses all technology; however, many U.S. companies do not link their superb technology to commercial applications and thus fail to develop new products. In the 1990s, the United States must take stock of its management style and techniques. The political leadership should contribute new ideas and programs, including the following:

- Reevaluate the labor contract system and consider adoption of lifetime employment.

- Stop encouraging workers in automobile factories and other plants to resign voluntarily, a disguised form of lay-off.
- Promote engineers to middle management.
- Hire employees on the basis of ability.
- Establish merit-pay systems and publicize commendations and awards for suggestions and creativity. The Deming Prize awarded in Japan for quality control is an example.
- Foster among employees a sense of common purpose with their company.
- Create loyalty and commitment to the company through extensive benefits and recreational programs and facilities.
- Reorganize unions to spur identification with their company. Consider establishing enterprise-level unions, which would be employees' primary affiliation, with a second tier of craft unions if necessary.
- Reconsider the terms of employment, root and branch, and provide security against layoffs, for example, to foster labor-management cooperation.
- Recognize that a corporation is privately owned but also a public entity with obligations to its employees and the public.
- Study tax measures to limit the huge bonuses paid to corporate executives.
- Stop the hemorrhaging of profits. Management bonuses are an appropriation of profits; they should come from gross profits and not be classified as an expense.
- Consider aggressive door-to-door sales campaigns instead of waiting for walk-in customers.
- Accept responsibility for employee training and provide suitable programs, for which the government should consider tax incentives.

- Encourage worker participation in management.
- Establish collective responsibility in the production and assembling process, with the goal of total quality control for every work team. Seek emulation of systems like Ford's "concurrent engineering" concept.

4. Regulatory Policy

In the spirit of GATT, the United States should abolish all regulations on exports and imports that restrain international trade and competition. Specific recommendations are as follows:

- Simplify the Coordinating Committee for Export Control (COCOM) and abolish restrictions on the reexport of certain items.
- End the ban on exporting Alaskan crude oil and natural gas.
- Consider abolition of "voluntary restraints" agreements by foreign exporters of steel, machine tools, and automobiles.
- Abolish the Super 301 provision of the 1988 Omnibus Trade and Competitiveness Act.
- Increase user taxes, especially on gasoline, and establish goal-specific taxes that the public will support.
- Reduce the speed limit to below fifty-five miles per hour.

5. Research and Development

To correct the imbalance between basic and applied research, the United States should provide additional funding and resources to the latter. Specific suggestions are as follows:

- Appropriate $71 billion for federally supported research and development in Fiscal Year (FY) 1991, allocating a portion to the National Science Foundation.

- Raise and extend tax deductions for corporate research and experimentation.
- Consider adoption of the metric system by all organizations that set technical standards.
- Shift research and development budget priorities from armaments to civilian products.
- Design policies to promote applied and product-development research.
- To the extent possible without detriment to U.S. national interests, cooperate with Japan in space exploration.
- Encourage joint development projects with Japan through mutual technological exchange.
- Increase budget allocations for science and engineering education and robotics.

6. *Export Promotion*

In today's global economy, the United States must devise more effective export-promotion measures. In particular:

- Prepare detailed export programs for Japan and other countries.
- Allocate $159 million for federal export promotions in FY 1991.
- Create a Foreign Trade Promotion Corporation, with public and private participation, to conduct market research and advise exporters.
- Adopt new trade indices. The current system of statistics is impractical and misleading.
- Provide goods targeted for specific foreign markets, such as automobiles with right-hand drive for Japan.
- Establish a permanent U.S.-Japan forum for bilateral dialogue.

- Stop the exclusive import-agent system, which inflates the price of U.S. products in Japan, and establish sales companies.
- Develop industries that will benefit other countries and promote export of their products.

7. Education

The American worker's low level of basic skills is a major reason for the decline of U.S. industry. Rectifying this deficiency should be the highest priority, bar none, and will require a multifaceted approach, including major funding increases. Other suggestions include:

- Allocate 5 percent of the GNP to education.
- Set objectives to be attained by the year 2000, such as a 90 percent graduation rate for high schools, top scores in comparative international tests in mathematics and science, and 100 percent adult literacy.
- Shift a portion of the cost of education from local communities to the federal government.
- Encourage state and local initiatives.
- From Head Start classes through graduate school, instill in students the traditional American spirit of self-reliance.
- Emphasize engineering and natural science in higher education.

8. Worker Education and Training

Each company is responsible for the attitude and basic skills of its employees. U.S. companies should undertake the following initiatives:

- Consider tax relief for intracompany education.
- Increase on-the-job training.
- Establish public vocational training institutes.
- Encourage American and Japanese entry-level workers to participate in corporate training programs in each other's country.

9. National Security and Foreign Aid

Political changes in the Soviet Union and Eastern Europe have inspired a worldwide reexamination of national priorities and objectives. U.S. strategy should reflect the new realities and make America strong again. Specifically, the following suggestions should be considered:

- Curb the special privileges and vested interests of the professional military and the Pentagon by reducing positions and personnel.
- Reduce nuclear weapons to the minimum.
- Slash U.S. overseas forces and bases. For example, commercial air facilities in the Tokyo area—Haneda Airport and the New Tokyo International Airport—are strained to the danger point. For the safety and convenience of domestic and foreign travelers, the U.S. government should promptly return the little-used Yokota Air Base in western Tokyo. This transfer would be welcomed by the Japanese public and have a very positive effect on bilateral relations.
- Strive for joint weapons development with Japan, not as a way to reduce the trade imbalance but on the basis of each country sharing technology. Such projects should enable Japan to make a greater contribution to mutual security and lighten the U.S. burden.

- Use weapons and equipment procurement funds more efficiently.
- Eliminate collusion between industry and the military in defense contracts.
- In accordance with the increases in Japan's own self-defense capability, conduct a qualitative and quantitative review of the mutual security treaty.
- To make Official Development Assistance to foreign countries more effective, create a joint Japan-U.S. consultative committee and formulate a global aid strategy.
- Allow Japan a free hand with its own Official Development Assistance program.

10. A Safer, Sounder American Society

The public and private sector must work together to reduce crime and devise new urban politics. Specifically:

- Control guns and drugs and educate the public against their use.
- Stiffen penalties for crimes of sexual abuse, particularly those involving children.
- Ban strikes by the police.
- Establish neighborhood "police boxes" (*koban*). Many parts of Washington, D.C., are so dangerous that tourists are afraid to visit them. There are no such areas in Japan because police are stationed in the community.
- Improve public transportation to lessen dependence on private automobiles.

Epilogue

I VISITED Washington, D.C., from January 15 to January 20, 1990, to correct misunderstandings caused by the vile, error-filled pirate translation of the Japanese edition of my book and to fulfill many requests for meetings and interviews. During my brief stay, I gave six television interviews and met with reporters from *The New York Times*, *The Washington Post*, the *Los Angeles Times*, *The Wall Street Journal*, the *Chicago Tribune*, and the Associated Press.

I also had lively exchanges with Secretary of Commerce Robert Mosbacher, Senators Richard Lugar and Jeff Bingaman, and Congressmen Richard Gephardt and Sander Levin. My aide told me that journalists were surprised that I was able to get appointments with Mosbacher and Gephardt. Perhaps they were curious about this "strange" fellow from Tokyo.

The masochistic Japanese press called my sojourn a "pilgrimage of apology," implying that I was a penitent seeking forgiveness. Far from it. I made no excuses and tried to press home my arguments. On January 19, *The Washington Post* headlined a story, "Fiery Words from Japan."

A Japanese Gephardt Goes to Washington

Richard Gephardt is a major congressional critic of Japan and advocates sanctions against our products. He is a high-powered politician who is not afraid to speak his mind. "I'm the Japanese Gephardt," I told him when we met. He laughed heartily, breaking the tension, and we had a friendly talk.

Sander Levin is a Democrat from Michigan. We met for lunch and, at first, he was insufferable, making angry remarks about the "awful" Japanese government. For four years, he said, U.S. companies have requested Japanese car makers to purchase American-made spark plugs, to no avail. In my view, the real problem is that American companies will not redesign the plugs to meet Japanese standards. When I raised the FSX issue, calling the conditions imposed on Japan the equivalent of an unequal treaty, Levin was at a loss for words. Finally, he said, "Please understand, Mr. Ishihara, that the FSX issue arose in the context of the U.S. trade deficit with Japan."

Members of Congress only meet Japanese who smile and agree with them, I suspect. I was the first one who ever countered their charges with Japan's own grievances. One TV reporter was so nonplussed at my directness, unlike any other Japanese she had interviewed, that she discarded her list of prepared questions.

Many American politicians and journalists who had not fully appreciated the implications of the FSX project were upset at my remarks. I also touched on other issues that Japan—the government and business community—had not vigorously addressed. The visit reinforced my belief in the importance of frank discussion between our two countries. In Japan, I am considered something of a bull in a china shop, but Americans like someone who does not mince words. And I believe that open, honest talks will be crucial to the Japan-U.S. relationship in the 1990s.

My meeting with Mosbacher was very contentious, mainly over the FSX. I told him that Japan should have rejected all the unfair conditions of the agreement. As I mentioned earlier, the United States required inter alia that Japan pay license fees for technology, but not the United States, and imposed unequal terms for civilian applications of technology. Mosbacher defended the inequalities by saying, "The value of the U.S. and Japanese technology is different. We spent vast amounts of money over forty years to acquire ours. None of the Japanese technology is original. It's not comparable to America's." We were talking past each other on this point. The Commerce Department's position is that Japan should buy more from the United States, anything that is cheap and of good quality, and stop caviling.

I do not advocate domestic production of the FSX to save money. As should be clear by now, developing our own fighter, one suited to Japan's peculiar security needs, even if it is more expensive than purchasing American models off the shelf, would help restore our national identity, increase our psychological and technological independence, and reduce America's burden for regional defense. Most American politicians and journalists that I talked with could see the logic of this, but not Mosbacher.

Attacks and Rebuttal

Americans were most disturbed about my views on racial prejudice. I had written that racial prejudice underlies Japan-bashing and many Americans I met denied this. One insisted that American society was virtually free of racism. "The day you arrived in Washington was a national holiday in honor of Martin Luther King, Jr.," he said. "Have you ever read Lincoln's Emancipation Proclamation?"

"I am well aware of both," I replied. "But didn't Americans have slaves longer than other Caucasians? Because Lincoln belatedly freed them doesn't change the fact that America continued slavery long after any European country. It's fine to honor Dr. King," I added, "but wasn't he killed by a white man?" He dropped the subject.

In response to my comments about bias, another American said, "We are prejudiced. We know that. But don't make such an issue of it."

I declined to be silent. "If there is racism in America," I said, "shouldn't you face it and fight it? Trying to overcome bigotry is important."

I have asked many American friends—people of mixed races, Orientals, Indians, and blacks—"Do Caucasians treat you with respect?" They laughed at the very idea. No one is completely free of prejudice. That being the human condition, it is far better to bring the issue out in the open and change outlooks.

"That's right," Americans say, "but you're touching a very sensitive nerve. We are trying to end racism, so stop making these inflammatory statements."

The American melting pot is a failed experiment. Racial discrimination may be a taboo topic there, but it is not for me. I said Japanese are probably prejudiced, too. "Rather than make excuses, we should try to overcome these attitudes." And I told Americans that Japan should be more responsive to the boat people and adopt a more flexible policy toward illegal unskilled Asian workers in the country.

The other point Americans brought up was the comment in my book that the global military balance could be completely upset if Japan decided to sell its computer chips to the Soviet Union instead of the United States. My point was that Japan's electronics industry is an irreplaceable asset to U.S. global strategy. This statement is probably what prompted the Pentagon to have the book translated.

In addition, many Americans said that the content and tone of the book were "nationalistic," an infuriating allegation. When I asked them to elaborate, the standard reply was that the book was infused with "nationalistic, racial self-righteousness." I countered, "It's not self-righteousness. My purpose was to enhance bilateral cooperation. When America is in the wrong, it should mend its ways."

In any case, my views were often misunderstood because of the abysmally translated pirate edition of my book. There were flagrant errors and some parts were deleted, apparently to distort my position. My statement that Japan should not reject all American trade demands and must not allow special interest groups to exclude foreign products was omitted. A possibly offensive line was also dropped: "Americans, with their scant few centuries of history, have never experienced the shift from one major historical period to another."

On my second day in Washington, Pentagon spokesman Pete Williams told a press conference that the Defense Advanced Research Projects Agency had had the book translated. They had used a Japanese translator, he said, and because the material was intended for internal use only and not for public dissemination, there was no copyright infringement.

The media asked me what I intended to do, and I said I would seek legal advice. I now know who to sue, and since I have suffered financial loss, I intend to seek redress. Copies of the pirated version reportedly were selling for $600 each. In Seattle, Washington, the downtown public library had several copies and readers were making their own on the library's copier. Does not this violate my copyright?

Redefining the Japan-U.S. Relationship

Two objective studies that I mentioned earlier, the Young
report and *Made in America,* have catalogued the weaknesses
of American industry that must be corrected if the country is
to regain international competitiveness. The United States
accuses Japan of unfair trading practices, but the Young report notes that the more open the Japanese market becomes,
the more efficient Japanese manufacturers will be. During an
exchange on CBS television, an irritated reporter asked,
"Then you and Mr. Morita are saying the United States should
learn from Japan?"

"No, I do not say that," I responded. "Have you read the
MIT book and the Young report? They are excellent. Many
American businessmen and scholars know what to do. Listen
to them. That's the way the United States can come back.
Why can't you learn from yourselves?"

Very few Americans, including politicians, seem to be fa-
miliar with these publications. The people I met think the
U.S. trade deficit is entirely Japan's fault. Japan bears only
partial responsibility for the bilateral trade imbalance. Not all
the American demands are misguided or irrational, however.
Trade Representative Carla Hills is correct about rigged bidding and other closed aspects of the Japanese market, and we
should respond affirmatively in these areas. Not because the
United States is demanding changes, of course. Such reforms
would also serve the interests of Japanese consumers and
taxpayers.

As I noted in the book, a 1989 Economic Planning Agency
report showed that prices were 40 percent higher in Tokyo
than in New York, with items subject to government control
especially expensive. Quick deregulation would give consumers a much deserved break.

There is also endemic collusion among bureaucrats, industries, and politicians in Japan. The costs of large-scale public works projects like high-speed train lines, harbor facilities, and airports are inflated by 15 to 20 percent through secret discussions among a few general contractors. These firms skim hundreds of millions of dollars from contracts and give vast sums to politicians in return for influence. The Japanese taxpayers should not tolerate this mutual back scratching.

I spoke out against former prime minister Tanaka Kakuei many years ago because he was involved in such flagrant abuses. This system must be destroyed. Here is a case where we can say yes to Washington and help the Japanese public.

But it is ultimately up to the United States to reduce its trade deficit. During my visit, U.S. trade figures for November 1989 were released, showing the worst one-month deficit of the year. I told American politicians that I personally would do my best to spur market-opening measures and would discuss SII with like-minded colleagues in Japan. I coupled that assurance with a warning: "Under present circumstances, opening the Japanese market to foreign goods will strengthen our industry."

Whether American products can win in competition on what Washington loves to call a "level playing field" depends on the efforts of American management. The prescription for recovery is in the Young report and *Made in America.*

Trans-Pacific Discourse

In the original book and in January, I talked straight from the shoulder to Americans. Some were not ready for my unvarnished comments and seemed offended. But open discourse is a good starting point for redefining the bilateral relationship between the United States and Japan. All the American politicians I met agreed with me on the need for more face-to-face contact. I suggested that we establish a forum where Japanese and U.S. legislators can discuss trade, farm exports, defense, etc., and work for a more constructive relationship. Regular meetings of lawmakers—parliamentary summits—would be very useful. The first could be a debate, open to the media, in Washington.

In addition to trade problems, legislators in both countries should reexamine the Japan-U.S. security treaty in the light of current realities. The choice is not all-or-nothing—abrogate or keep the unequal arrangements. Yet Washington is very reluctant to modify the present understanding.

I believe we are now strong enough technologically and financially to create an independent, defensive military force. Thus, it is time to think about a security pact in which Japan would have more to say. The United States must accept that reality and Japan must make a larger contribution to mutual security. Elected representatives in both countries should address this issue.

My January trip cleared the air and perhaps won a few converts. By avoiding the bland pap that usually passes for international exchange, we got to the core issues in a stimulating, satisfying way. During my May trip, I also spoke to an attentive and receptive audience. I hope that future Japan-U.S. dialogue will be equally fruitful.

Translator's Note

Despite the Biblical admonition and against common sense, the translator tries to serve two masters. On the one hand, authors expect total transmission of their ideas. They want every deft simile and subtle nuance in place. The inchoate phrase must be made whole, the in-joke rendered humorous to outsiders, the sarcastic fillip delivered like a left jab. On the other hand, readers demand instant access to a different mindset and culture. They want textual fidelity worthy of Caesar's wife presented in a seductively natural prose style. No trace of the original may remain but neither may anything be "lost in translation." With no Solomonic solution available, the translator struggles on, aware that these potential nemeses, skeptical about the transcultural process, will be looking over his or her shoulder.

The hostile firestorm that greeted the original Morita and Ishihara book in the United States, through the existence of a pirated English translation (a contemptible piece of work), made me unusually sensitive to the scrutiny in store for the authorized version. Not only will a legion of Japan-bashers pore over the American edition for signs that Shintaro Ishihara has toned down his opinions, but many curious people will compare it with the original to see how controversial or ambiguous passages were treated. Both sets of readers should be interested to know that my brief from the author was clear: Do a professional job and scrupulously preserve the integrity of the Japanese text, lest critics claim that there has been modification or even deceit.

Thus, the author relinquished his right to make the substantial revisions of Part I that would usually be done upon publication of a translation, and I lost a certain freedom of expression.

I wish to acknowledge the assistance of Tsutomu Kano, my longtime mentor and colleague, who solved countless linguistic and stylistic puzzles. For failure to heed his advice and any errors that remain, I bear responsibility.

FRANK BALDWIN

Index

151